Sports Roots

BOOKS BY HARVEY FROMMER

Sports Roots   (1979)

Sports Lingo   (1979)

The Martial Arts: Judo and Karate   (1978)

A Sailing Primer (WITH RON WEINMANN)   (1978)

*A Baseball Century: The First Hundred Years
    of the National League*   (1976)

SPORTS ROOTS

How Nicknames, Namesakes, Trophies, Competitions, and Expressions in the World of Sports Came to Be

HARVEY FROMMER

ATHENEUM   *1979*   *New York*

The photographs which follow pages 61 and 121 are reproduced by courtesy of PHOTOWORLD, 110 West 32nd Street, New York City, except for the photograph of Pele, which is by courtesy of the Pepsi-Cola Company.

The excerpt from *Death of a Salesman* by Arthur Miller, Copyright 1949 by Arthur Miller, Copyright © renewed 1977 by Arthur Miller, is reprinted by permission of Viking Penguin Inc.

Library of Congress Cataloging in Publication Data

Frommer, Harvey.
  Sports roots.

  1. Sports—Miscellanea.   2. Sports—Terminology.
3. Sports—Slang.   I. Title.
GV706.8.F76 1979   796   79-9729
ISBN 0-689-10980-6

TO CAROLINE
for rooting

WILLY: Yeah, heh? When this game is over, Charley, you'll be laughing out of the other side of your face. They'll be calling him another Red Grange. Twenty-five thousand a year . . .

CHARLEY: Well, then, I'm sorry, Willy. But tell me something.

WILLY: What?

CHARLEY: Who is Red Grange?

WILLY: Put up your hands. Goddam you, put up your hands!

ARTHUR MILLER, *Death of a Salesman,* Act II

ACKNOWLEDGMENTS

A work of this sort would never have surfaced without the encouragement, criticism, assistance, and presence of a number of people. Thank you Jennifer ("J"), Freddy ("Fred-Boy"), Ian ("Big E"), and Paul Sigler.

For shaping and faith—thank you Marvin Brown of Atheneum. Robert Hendrickson and his fine work *Human Words* proved to be very helpful, as did the sensitive copy editing of Dan Flanagan.

The largest thanks is owed to my wife, Myrna, whose patience and talent helped fuel the entire effort.

H. F.

INTRODUCTION

Language has miraculous power. It transforms, elevates, glamorizes, even immortalizes. How super would the Super Bowl be if it were called by some other name? Would Jersey Joe Walcott have had the same image if he went through all his life being called by his real name—Arnold Cream? The St. Louis Cardinals of the 1930's were an exciting baseball team. How much more exciting and enduring have they become because of the "Gashouse Gang" phrase used to describe them?

The "Mad Hungarian" is more intimidating than Al Hrabosky. The "Barber" was more ferocious than Sal Maglie. "Clyde" was cooler than Walt Frazier. Jerome Hannah Dean was never as glamorous and exciting as "Dizzy" Dean was. Pete Maravich suggests one image; "Pistol Pete" Maravich is something entirely different. "To play this game [baseball] you've got to have a lot of little boy in you." There have been hundreds of thousands of words written to characterize the national pastime. Very few of these words have said as much about baseball as Roy Campanella's sentence.

For those involved with the world of sports, and for many others, the names, nicknames, expressions, competitions that form the language of the sports scene are terms of familiarity. The language is above all one of connotation. Although much of the language has roots in press agentry, in hype, in commercial convenience, or in another time, much of the language has survived and mellowed, become more appealing.

This book is an attempt to survey and probe how these "sportsnyms" came to be. It is a selective collection of fakirs and fakers; innovators and imitators; the vain, the vanquished, the vital; achievers and underachievers. "Reds" and "Lefties," "Bobos" and "Whiteys" have been omitted, as well as dozens of Campbells nicknamed Soupy and Rhodes dubbed "Dusty."

What has been included is the Stanley Cup, named for a donator who never witnessed a Stanley Cup game; the bat named for a city named for a French king; the trophy named for the schooner named for the nation that has always won the cup; the race named for a rock; the baseball commissioner whose name was derived in part from the Civil War mountain battle-site where his father was wounded.

The "Stilt" is here, as is the Italian word for *stilt* that gave its name to a gymnastic apparatus. Included also are the horse-racing derbies named for the earl who spent more time improving the breed than he did improving his relationship with his wife. These pages contain the Great White Hope and the Brown Bomber, the Black Babe Ruth and the Black Honus Wagner. Comic strip characters Gump (Worsley) and (Gravel) Gertie are here, too.

Sports Roots contains the football team named for a packing company, the baseball team that gained its name from the way its fans dodged trolleys, the baseball team tagged forever because of its alleged attempts to "steal" a player. The nickname that wasn't wanted and the one that was patented, the tights that bear the name of its vain inventor, the boxing division originated by the manager of its first champion, the sport named as a result of the passion for hunting of two baseball Hall of Famers—all of these and more are in these pages.

There's a silver fox, a rabbit, a wild bull, a horse, a wild horse, an eagle, a penguin, an antelope, a crab, a crow. There are Giants and giants, dwarfs and fat people, a rajah, a duke, an earl, a sultan, a clown prince. The world's most famous nickname is here, as is the splendid irony of its bearer not knowing what his nickname means or how he got it.

How polo, basketball, soccer, softball, Little League baseball, Ping-Pong, volleyball, the Rose Bowl, the Super Bowl, rodeo, ice dancing, and more began and earned their names—these too are included.

Like faded playbooks, yellowing programs, and tattered token tickets, many of the terms, nicknames, trophies, and competitions of sports suggest another feeling about ourselves and our world. Other terms are as timely as today's newspaper. An attempt has been made to mesh the exotic with the ordinary, the old with the new, the poignant with the humorous, to make for an October offering for the sports fan, the trivia and nostalgia buff, the language aficionados . . . and all those who like to get at the root of things.   H. F.

Sports Roots

A

ADMIRAL'S CUP Named for its presenter (the admiral) and other members of the Royal Ocean Racing Club (RORC), this cup originated in 1957. It is an international trophy for which teams of three boats from different nations compete when they participate in the Fastnet, Britannia Cup, Channel Race, and New York Yacht Club Race.

ALABAMA ANTELOPE, THE Don Hutson came from the Rose Bowl–winning University of Alabama football team to the Green Bay Packers of the National Football League in 1935. He stayed for 11 seasons; nine times he was named All-Pro. Hutson's nickname came from his collegiate alma mater and the blazing speed and deceptive moves he was able to unleash as a pro. Named an all-time All-Pro in 1970, Hutson caught nearly 500 passes in his pro career, and almost one out of five of those receptions resulted in a touchdown.

ALL-AMERICAN Walter Camp's name is always identified with the idea of selecting college football All-
Americans. However, credit for the original idea be-
longs to Caspar W. Whitney, a part-owner of *This
Week's Sport* magazine, who approached Camp with
the concept. Both Camp and Whitney chose the All-
Americans for 1889 and 1890. *This Week's Sport* then
ceased publication. Whitney joined *Harper's Weekly*
and from 1891 to 1896 picked All-American teams for
that publication. Camp picked the 1897 team for
Harper's Weekly. In 1898 Camp began a long career
with *Collier's,* selecting All-American teams until his
death in 1925. While with *Collier's,* Camp listed the
All-Americans from 1889 on and thus created the im-
pression that he was the one responsible for the "All-
American" concept, while Whitney actually deserves
the credit.

ALL-STAR GAME (BASEBALL) The idea was conceived
in 1933 by Arch Ward, Chicago *Tribune* sports editor.
To give the fans a real rooting interest, Ward suggested
that they be allowed to vote for their favorite players
via popular ballot. In perhaps no other game do fans
have such a rooting interest, although there have been
a few periods when voting by fans has been aban-
doned. Today it appears that Ward's original principle
will remain permanently in effect. The American
League won 12 of the first 16 All-Star games, but went
on to lose 20 of the next 23 to the National League
through 1978. Some memorable moments have taken
place in the contest often referred to as the Midsummer

Dream Game. In the first game ever played, Babe Ruth slugged a towering home run. The next year, New York Giants immortal Carl Hubbell struck out Babe Ruth, Lou Gehrig, Jimmy Foxx, Al Simmons, and Joe Cronin in succession to make for some more baseball history.

ALL-WORLD Lloyd Free, National Basketball Association free soul, who learned his basketball on the sidewalks of New York, gave himself this nickname. Free is a little man in a world of giants, and a comparative unknown in a world where most players have press agents and exotic nicknames. Free considers himself and his "rainbow shot," which goes high in the air and down at the basket, worthy of the nickname he dreamed up.

AMAZIN' METS The first run they ever scored came in on a balk. They lost the first nine games they ever played. They finished last their first four seasons. Once they were losing a game, 12-1, and there were two outs in the bottom of the ninth inning. A fan held up a sign that said "PRAY!" There was a walk, and ever hopeful, thousands of voices chanted, "Let's go Mets." They were 100-1 underdogs to win the pennant in 1969 and incredibly came on to finish the year as World Champions. They picked the name of the best pitcher in their history (Tom Seaver) out of a hat on April Fools' Day. They were supposed to be the replacement for the Brooklyn Dodgers and the New York Giants. They could have been the New York Continentals or Burros or Skyliners or Skyscrapers or Bees or Rebels or NYB's or Avengers or even Jets (all runner-up names in a contest to tab the National League New York team that began playing ball in 1962). They've never been anything to their fans but amazing—the Amazin' New York Mets.

AMBLING ALP Allegedly the inspiration for the book and movie *The Harder They Fall* by Budd Schulberg, Primo Carnera was also allegedly discovered functioning as a strongman in a touring European circus. He was nearly 300 pounds of man and at 6'6" was an impressive fighting figure. However, he was more of a human punching-bag than a pro boxer. Carnera was knocked down 11 times in 11 rounds by Max Baer and suffered similar losses to other fighters. The fights he won were allegedly fixed. His nickname came from his size and his lack of any style or movement in the ring.

AMERICAN ICE MASTER Jackson Haines revolutionized the sport of ice skating, and because of his contributions he was given his nickname. A United States ballet master, Haines went to Austria when the Civil War began. In Vienna he fused the Austrian interests in skating and in the waltz into a new form of ice skating. Haines invented dancing on ice, teaching and demonstrating how skaters could glide, spiral, twist, and synchronize their moves with music. He also introduced all manner of novelty gyrations on skates, including skating on stilts. In 1875, after his death, Finland erected a monument that paid tribute to Haines as the "American Skating King."

AMERICA'S CUP The Royal Yacht Club of England in 1851 donated a trophy, originally called the Hundred-Guinea Cup, that was to go to the winner of a race around the Isle of Wight. The yacht race was a part of the ceremonies of the London Exposition of that year. Valued at about $500, the cup was won by a United States schooner named *America,* which defeated 14 British yachts. The British were not too impressed with the American accomplishment and maintained that they would "in due time" get back the cup. As the competition evolved, the trophy was given to the New York Yacht Club for permanent and perpetual international competition and has been presented to the champions of a series of international races for 12-meter yachts. The America's Cup still remains—as it always has—in the United States. More than $75,000,000 has been expended in attempting to win the cup named for the vessel named for the nation that originally won the trophy.

ARNIE'S ARMY Excitable yet restrained when they must be, loyal but at times critical, those fans who through the years have followed golfer Arnold Palmer over hill and dale have earned their nickname. Some have even said that their presence has at times lent an extra dimension of support to Palmer's game.

ASTROTURF Not all of the artificial carpets that now have taken root in ball parks and stadiums in the United States and around the world are produced by the Monsanto Chemical Company. AstroTurf was the first, however, having been installed when the Houston Astrodome opened in 1965, and that's why the term has almost become a generic one for artificial sod. There is also Tartan Turf (made by Minnesota Mining and Manufacturing) and Poly-Turf (a product of American

Bilt-Rite). Resistant to all types of weather, more efficient to keep up than grass, better for traction than most other surfaces, synthetic "grass" has continued to "grow" throughout the world of sports, despite complaints that it results in more injuries for players. Studies focused on injuries are still in progress, while other research is under way aimed at improving the quality of the artificial carpets.

AUSTRALIAN TAG-TEAM WRESTLING Promoter Jack Pfeffer originated the idea of Australian tag-team wrestling during World War II. The aged, the out-of-shape, the inexperienced, and the unskilled wrestlers available for bouts during the war—for the able-bodied were taking part in the war effort—proved to be the inspiration for Pfeffer's promotion. Television helped fuel the public's interest and this hybrid version of wrestling is still popular today. It involves a fatigued wrestler being relieved by his partner if he is able to tag that partner, who is stationed at a corner of the ring.

AVCO WORLD TROPHY The World Hockey Association's best-of-seven-games championship series is named for AVCO Financial Services, the league's major sponsor and donor. The first championship, in 1973, was won by the New England Whalers.

B

BABE, THE Called Monk or Monkey by many of his opponents, Jidge by the great majority of his teammates, the Sultan of Swat by some overreaching sportswriters, George Herman Ruth, also known as the Bambino, was The Babe to most baseball fans of his time. His main nickname was rooted in President Cleveland's Baby Ruth. Perhaps the greatest slugger of all time and also one of baseball's most colorful characters, Ruth set some 50 records in his 22 years as a player. His accomplishments, his personality, his nickname—all combined to rocket major league baseball firmly into the nation's psyche.

BABE RUTH OF HOCKEY Eddie Shore of the National Hockey League Boston Bruins played for almost two decades, picking up nearly one thousand stitches in a brawling, no-holds-barred career. A defenseman who skated the length of the ice when the occasion demanded it, a crowd pleaser on his home ice and a target for fans on the road, Shore was a seven-time All-Star and four-time Most Valuable Player. He made people notice hockey in the same way Babe Ruth made people notice baseball, and that was a part of the reason for his nickname. Former Boston trainer Hammy Moore offered another reason: "Eddie was the only player I ever saw who had the whole arena standing every time he rushed down the ice . . . when he carried the puck you were always sure something would happen. He would either end up bashing somebody, get into a fight, or score a goal."

BADMINTON A game called poona was developed in India and then allegedly came to Great Britain by way of British Army officers who had played it during their leisure hours. In 1873 the Duke of Beaufort staged a party at his country manor, Badminton. Poona, or the English version of the sport, was played with slightly rearranged rules. The streamlined version of poona played at Badminton was the root of the sport as we know it today.

BADMINTON HORSE TRIALS This three-day event was originated in Great Britain in 1952 by another Duke of Beaufort. Named for its site—his park at Badminton, Gloucestershire—the competition seeks to raise the quality of British horsemanship. Dressage, a 17-mile speed and endurance test, and show jumping are the three events. The winner is the rider with the highest point total.

BANTAMWEIGHT In the 1880's, when organized boxing was young and innocent, the smallest competitors were called little chickens or bantams, after the fowl of the same name. These fighters could go at each other for hours at a time and although they were bantams, they were anything but little chickens. The original bantamweights weighed 105 pounds, then 112, 116, and today, 118.

BARBER, THE Sal Maglie had the unique distinction of pitching for the Brooklyn Dodgers, the New York Yankees and the New York Giants in the 1950's. A curveballing clutch pitcher, his nickname came from two sources. A swarthy 6'2" righthander who always seemed to need a shave, he was a master at "shaving" or "barbering" the plate. His pitches would nick the corner, and he wasn't too shy about nicking a batter if the occasion demanded it.

BARON, THE A strong-minded individual whose Kentucky teams rank among the greatest in the history of college basketball, Adolph Rupp's nickname came from his imperial manner and his record of success. "I know I have plenty of enemies," he once said, "but I'd rather be the most hated winning coach in the country than the most popular losing one." Rupp's teams made more appearances in the NCAA tournament than any other coach's; he produced more than two dozen All-Americans, and he ranks on top of the list of all-time winning college coaches.

BARTER This English cricket term has its roots in the skilled performance of Robert Barter, warden at Winchester College (1832–61). Barter was famous for his half-volley hits—the shot that the term bearing his name denotes.

BASEBALL CARDS About 20 years before the American League was organized in 1901, the first baseball cards appeared. Photographs were taken in an artist's studio. Action was simulated to approximate game conditions: the baseballs that players apparently were hitting were suspended from the ceiling by a string, and the bases that players were shown sliding into were actually set into a wooden floor. These early baseball cards were printed on paper with sepia tone and included in packs of cigarettes from the leading companies of that era: Old Judge, Piedmont, Sweet Caporal, Polar Bear, and Recruit. Bubble-gum baseball cards originated in 1933 with cards made of heavy cardboard and averaging about 2½″ × 3″. Their popularity grew until World War II caused a halt in their production. In 1951 Topps entered the baseball-card field and has continued to innovate and dominate the market.

The most valuable baseball card in existence is a 1910 Honus Wagner that was issued by the Sweet Caporal Tobacco Company. Wagner did not smoke and objected to the use of his name and image on a card; therefore, all the Wagner cards were removed from circulation except for the seven known to exist today. They are each valued as high as $1,500. The most valuable Topps card is a 1952 Mickey Mantle. Issued only locally, the card is valued as high as $100. The largest collection of baseball cards is housed in New York City's Metropolitan Museum of Art—over 200,000 cards make up the collection.

BAT DAY In 1951 Bill Veeck ("as in wreck") owned the
St. Louis Browns, a team that was not the greatest gate
attraction in the world. (It's rumored that one day a fan
called up Veeck and asked, "What time does the game
start?" Veeck's alleged reply was, "What time can you
get here?") Veeck was offered six thousand bats at a
nominal fee by a company that was going bankrupt. He
took the bats and announced that a free bat would be
given to each youngster attending a game accompanied
by an adult. That was the beginning of Bat Day. Veeck
followed this promotion with Ball Day and Jacket Day
and other giveaways. Bat Day, Ball Day, and Jacket
Day have all become virtually standard major league
baseball promotions.

BEAUFORT SCALE Devised in 1805 by British Rear Admiral Sir Francis Beaufort, the scale that bears his
name indicates wind strength. Forces range from 0 to
17. Force 0 signifies calm; Force 1, light air (1–3
MPH); Force 2, slight breeze (4–7 MPH); Force 3,
gentle breeze (8–12 MPH); Force 4, moderate breeze
(13–18 MPH); Force 5, fresh breeze (19–24 MPH);
Force 6, strong breeze (25–31 MPH); Force 7, moderate gale (32–38 MPH); Force 8, fresh gale (39–46
MPH); Force 9, strong gale (47–54 MPH); Force 10,
whole gale (55–63 MPH); Force 11, storm (64–73
MPH); and the numbers 12–17 represent hurricane
forces (74 MPH and more).

BELMONT PARK/BELMONT STAKES August Belmont
was a millionaire improver of the breed, the owner of
Whirlaway and breeder of Man o' War. The oldest and
largest racetrack in the United States, Belmont Park in

New York City, bears his name. The Belmont Stakes, held annually since 1867, is named for the track that is named for the millionaire. The Belmont Stakes, a 1½-mile race run in June for three-year-old thoroughbreds, is the third race in the Triple Crown of horse racing.

GORDON BENNETT CUP Named for the famed American publisher who presented it, this cup symbolized the winning of an international auto race for teams of three cars manufactured entirely in the country that entered them in competition. The races were staged in the years 1899–1905 and were ultimately supplanted by the Grand Prix (see GRAND PRIX).

BERMUDA RACE This sailing event originated in 1923 and is cosponsored by the Cruising Club of America and the Royal Bermuda Yacht Club. A race from New York to Bermuda, it alternates with the Fastnet, being held in even-numbered years (see FASTNET, THE).

BIG "D" The city of Dallas, Texas, and the National Football League team that represents the city, the Cowboys, do things in a big way. Computer-dominated, adorned with colorful star players, bedecked with some weird fans and lovely and shapely females who function as cheerleaders, the Cowboys of the NFL tower over most teams in prestige and performance—earning them their nickname.

BIG "D" His playing weight was 210 pounds and he stood 6'5". That partially accounted for former Dodger pitcher Don Drysdale's nickname. The rest stemmed from his nearly 2,500 career strikeouts, his more than two hundred games won, and the power pitching he was capable of during a 14-year career. Perhaps Drysdale's finest accomplishment was a string of 58⅔ consecutive scoreless innings pitched.

BIG "E" At 6'9" and 230 pounds, Elvin Hayes is an intimidating performer in the NBA. The former University of Houston All-American, a fine shooter and rebounder, earned his nickname for his size, performance, and appeal. The "E" was also a more appealing shortening of his first name.

BIG ED Five Irish brothers excited the sporting world around the turn of the century. The brothers Delahanty were paced by Edward James, better known as Ed, best known as Big Ed; he was over six feet tall and weighed 170 pounds—large proportions for his time. On a July afternoon in 1896, he became the second player in history to stroke four home runs in one game. In a 16-year major league career, the Hall of Famer recorded 2,597 hits and a lifetime batting average of .346. Delahanty batted .410 to lead the National League in 1899, when he was a member of the Philadelphia Phillies, and his .376 average in 1902, when he was a member of the Washington team in the American League, was second only to Napoleon Lajorie's .378. Collectively, the brothers Delahanty (Joe, Jim, Frank, Tom, and Ed) played in the majors for 38 years—two years more than the lifetime of the most accomplished Delahanty, Ed, who died at the age of 36.

BIG EIGHT This term designates a collegiate athletic conference consisting of Missouri, Nebraska, Colorado, Oklahoma, Oklahoma State, Kansas State, Kansas, and Iowa State.

BIG "O," THE Oscar Robertson was big at 6'5" and 205

pounds, but the nickname all of basketball knew him by came more from his big skills than his size. Robertson was a great shooter, a great passer, and a tremendous defensive player. Former Boston Celtic coach Red Auerbach once remarked, "He's so great he scares me. He can beat you all by himself and usually does." Robertson was selected to the All-Star team each year of his playing career and that was just another reason for his nickname—the Big "O" stood not for *zero,* but for *oh!*

BIG POISON and LITTLE POISON Paul Waner's rookie year with the Pittsburgh Pirates was 1926, when he batted .336 and led the league in triples. In one game he cracked out six hits using six different bats. In 1927 the second Waner arrived, brother Lloyd. For 14 years, the Waners formed a potent brother combination in the Pittsburgh lineup. Paul was 5'8½" and weighed 153 pounds. Lloyd was 5'9" and weighed 150 pounds. Paul was dubbed Big Poison even though he was smaller than Lloyd, who was called Little Poison. An older brother even then had privileges. But both players were pure poison for National League pitchers. Slashing left-handed line-drive hitters, the Waners collected 5,611 hits between them. Paul's lifetime batting average was .333, and he recorded three batting titles. Lloyd posted a career average of .316. They played a combined total of 38 years in the major leagues.

BIG RED MACHINE The Cincinnati Reds of the 1960's and middle 1970's were an offensive powerhouse. Sparked by Johnny Bench, Pete Rose, Tony Perez, and others, in one six-year span the club, with machinelike precision, produced an average of 95 wins a year.

BIG SIX, THE Christy Mathewson, 17 years a pitcher for the New York Giants (he also pitched one game for the Cincinnati Reds), was almost 6′2″ and weighed nearly 200 pounds. He wore uniform number 6. His fabled fadeaway pitch enabled the Hall of Famer to win 20 or more games 12 years in a row and 30 games in each of four years, three of those years in succession. The big blond with the number 6 on his back was one of the greatest pitchers in all of baseball history.

BIG SMOKE In 1908 Jack Johnson became the first black heavyweight champion of the world. A little over six feet tall, a little over 200 pounds, a little too flashy for his times—he wore mod clothes and drove yellow racing cars at high speed—Johnson was continually in trouble with the law because of brawling in public and reckless driving. His nickname was a grudging label for what he was. The "big" referred to his size. The "smoke" was that era's slang expression for a black person.

BIG TEN This term refers to the ten teams that make up the powerhouse midwestern collegiate athletic conference: Ohio State, Indiana, Illinois, Purdue, Iowa, Minnesota, Wisconsin, Michigan State, Northwestern, and Michigan. One team represents the conference annually in the Rose Bowl, where it competes against a college from the Pacific Ten.

BIG TRAIN Hall of Famer Walter Johnson led the majors in strikeouts 12 of his 21 years as a pitcher, notching a record 3,508. He pitched 113 shutout games, including a string of 56 straight scoreless innings from April 10

to May 14, 1913. Part of the reason for his nickname
was his seven shutout wins in seven opening-day
games, which moved his Washington Senator team off
down the track. Another reason for his nickname was
the almost mechanical precision of the 6'1", 200-
pound right-hander, who harnessed durability to power
in becoming one of baseball's immortals.

BILLIARDS The French word *billarts* or *billiard* ("cue
stick") is the derivation for the sport's name, but it was
English resourcefulness that gave birth to the sport.
Actually billiards began life as an indoor version of
lawn bowling, a game the English played with a
passion—only to have this passion frustrated when rain
fell on their beloved outdoor pastime. Thus the
Britishers moved the sport indoors. They built a table,
developed the use of a stick, and then a cue ball to
knock the ball into the appropriate pocket . . . and
with these innovations billiards came into being and
developed into one of the most scientific of the world's
games.

BITSY The diminutive size of Byran M. Grant earned him
his nickname. Just 120 pounds and a little over five
feet tall, Grant pound-for-pound and inch-for-inch was
one of the greatest tennis players of his time. Also
known as The Mighty Atom, Grant won the 1930,
1934, and 1935 National Clay Court Singles championships.

BLACK BELTS Professor Jigoro Kano, founder of judo,
originated the system of belts to clarify rankings in the
sport. The black belt symbolizes an expert, the white
belt is given to a beginner, and other colors reflect the
intermediate skills of judo practitioners.

BLACK BABE RUTH His name was Josh Gibson and he played at approximately the same time as Babe Ruth. A catcher in the Negro Leagues (1930–46), Gibson once hit a ball 580 feet in Yankee Stadium—the longest clout ever recorded there. In one four-year period Gibson notched 278 homers—and that was a major reason for his nickname.

BLACK GAZELLE Wilma Rudolph is one of the most graceful black women the world of sports has produced, and from that characteristic came her nickname. Unable even to walk at the age of seven, she won three gold medals in the 1960 Olympics, in the 100- and 200-meter dashes and as the anchor-runner in the 400-meter relay.

BLACK HONUS WAGNER John Henry "Pop" Lloyd and Honus Wagner were baseball contemporaries in the years 1906–17. Lloyd was a shortstop in the Negro Leagues who had few equals, while Wagner played the same role with the Pittsburgh Pirates of the National League. Not only did Lloyd and Wagner play at about the same time (Lloyd continued playing until 1931), but the way they played was similar. Both men were big, powerful hitters, excellent fielders, and smart base runners.

BLACK SOX In 1919 eight members of the Chicago White Sox were accused of conspiring to fix the World Series of that year. They were Shoeless Joe Jackson, Lefty Williams, Chick Gandil, Swede Risberg, Fred McMullin, Happy Felsch, Buck Weaver, and Eddie Cicotte. Williams won 23 games during the regular season; Cicotte won 29. In the World Series Williams lost three games and Cicotte two as the Reds defeated the

White Sox in five of the eight games played. Cicotte later admitted he was given $10,000 to "dump" the World Series. A 1920 grand jury investigation indicted the eight players, but before they had even been brought to trial they were banned for life from playing major league baseball. By 1921 seven of the players had been acquitted of the charges but the tarnishing and potentially damaging effect the allegations of a "fixed" World Series carried, resulted in this nickname for a whole team.

BLEACHER BUMS A self-named phenomenon of the late 1960's and early 1970's at Wrigley Field in Chicago, these were yellow–hard-hatted fans who swizzled beer and taunted opposing players while swearing allegiance to the Cubs. They functioned for a time as the tenth man on the Chicago Cubs team.

BLEACHERS Rows and rows of wooden bench-seats located in the most distant outreaches of stadiums, bleachers took their name from the effect that a dazzling summer sun can have on the bodies and clothes of diehard fans.

BLINKY This indelicate nickname was given to National Hockey League immortal Gordie Howe because of the slight facial tic an old injury gave him. In later years Howe was dubbed Old Blinky.

BOGEY In England around the turn of the century, a popular music-hall song exclaimed:

Hush! Hush! Hush!
Here comes the Bogey man!
So hide your head beneath the clothes,
He'll catch you if he can!

At the Coventry Club in 1890, each hole on the golf

course was given a scratch value—a *ground score* above par. The *bogey man* of the song became the *bogey* on the golf course—something to watch out for. In the United States, *bogey* eventually came to mean one stroke over par for a hole, *double bogey* to mean two strokes over par for a hole, etc.

BONEHEAD MERKLE The phrase "pulling a bonehead play," or "pulling a boner," is not only part of the language of baseball, but of all sports and in fact, of the language in general. Its most dramatic derivation goes back to September 9, 1908. Frederick Charles Merkle, a.k.a. George Merkle, was playing his first full game at first base for the New York Giants. It was his second season in the majors; the year before, he had appeared in 15 games. The Giants were in first place and the Cubs were challenging them. The two teams were tied, 1–1, in the bottom of the ninth inning. With two outs, the Giants' Moose McCormick was on third base and Merkle was on first. Al Bridwell slashed a single to center field, and McCormick crossed the plate with what was apparently the winning run. Merkle, eager to avoid the Polo Grounds crowd that surged onto the playing field, raced directly to the clubhouse instead of following through on the play and touching second base. Amid the pandemonium, Johnny Evers of the Cubs screamed for the baseball, obtained it somehow, stepped on second base, and claimed a force-out on Merkle. When things subsided, umpire Hank O'Day agreed with Evers. The National League upheld O'Day, Evers and the Cubs, so the run was nullified and the game not counted. Both teams played out their schedules and completed the season tied for first place with 98 wins and 55 losses. A replay of the game was scheduled, and Christy Mathewson, seeking his 38th victory of the season, lost, 4–2, to Three-Finger Brown *(q.v.)*. The Cubs won the pennant. Although Merkle played 16 years in the majors and had a lifetime batting average of .273, he will forever be rooted in sports lore as the man who made the "bonehead" play that lost the 1908 pennant for the Giants, for had he touched second base there would have been no replayed game and the Giants would have won the pennant by one game.

BOSEY This Australian cricket term originated in England and was taken from the name of the English bowler B. J. T. Bosanquet. He made famous the technique known as the googly when he toured Australia in 1903–04. Bowled with leg-break action, the googly is an off-break ball. Bosanquet's "bosey" thus is named for its inventor and one of its leading practitioners.

BOSTON MARATHON In 490 B.C. the Greeks defeated a much larger Persian army in a very significant battle. The news of the Greek victory was brought to Athens by a messenger who ran the 26 miles from the field of battle only to drop dead when he reached his destination. In 1897 the Boston Athletic Association inaugurated an annual international event that is staged each April. Individuals from all over the world compete in the 26-mile, 385-yard race that is run through the suburbs and city of Boston. The ancient Greek event and the locale of the race give it its name.

BOUDREAU SHIFT Named after Cleveland Indians manager Lou Boudreau, this was a radical shifting of four

infielders to the right side of the infield to counteract
the left-handed pull-hitting of Boston Red Sox star Ted
Williams.

BOWLING Judging from the enthusiasm and passion of
today's bowlers, it is not surprising that the sport began
life as a form of religious observance. In 4th-century
Germany, peasants fastidiously set up small clubs that
they called *kegels* in the cloisters of neighborhood
churches. The peasants then enthusiastically rolled
rounded stones at these kegels with the aim of knocking them down. A kegel symbolized a nonbeliever.
The knocking down of all the kegels was a sign of
arranging for good luck. Eventually the practice became a sport and spread to other nations. Bowling
Green in New York City owes its name to the sporting
efforts of the Dutch keglers of the 17th century who
brought the German 4th-century religious practice
along with them to America.

BOW WOW Henry Irven Arft played five years with the St.
Louis Browns in the late 1940's and early 1950's and
was a journeyman ball player. His nickname came
from the onomatopoeic sound of his last name.

BRASSIE This old term for the number 2 wood evolved
from the brass plate that was affixed to the sole of the
old wooden club. The plate's function was to offer
protection to a club when a player used it from a bad
lie.

BRAT, THE Eddie Stanky was a protégé of Leo Durocher. An infielder with limited skills, Stanky
played 11 years in the major leagues with five different
teams and compiled a lifetime batting average of .268.

He was also known as Muggsy, in tribute to his tough
guy, loud-mouthed playing characteristics (see "LIP,
THE").

BRM The designation given in 1950 to a series of British
Grand Prix racing cars, including, after 1963, a gas
turbine model. The initial letters of the last names of
the designers—P. Berthon and R. Mays—are included
in the name for the racing-car series.

BROADWAY JOE In 1964 the St. Louis Cardinals of the
National Football League and the New York Jets of the
American Football League, symbolizing the war of the
leagues for star players and television attractions, battled over the right to sign Alabama quarterback Joe
Namath. The American Football League and the Jets
won. Namath was signed to a four-year contract at
$25,000 a season plus a $200,000 bonus. Scouting
jobs were provided for his three brothers and a
brother-in-law at $10,000 a year. A green Lincoln
Continental plus other luxury features were included in
the deal, which totaled approximately $427,000. What
was called the Namath Effect was now set. His skills
on the playing field virtually assured the merger of the
AFL and the NFL, and he paced the Jets and the AFL
in 1969 to a Super Bowl III victory over the Baltimore
Colts, the National Football League representative.

Off the field Namath was showcased with glamorous
starlet types, with the Manhattan skyline as his
backdrop and the saloons and penthouses of New York
City as his resting places. An affable, charming, out-
going man, Namath attracted the ardor of women and
the envy of men. He was well publicized, and his

nickname was a well-earned appellation for him and for the mystique of the Big Apple.

BROCKTON BLOCKBUSTER Born in 1923 in Brockton, Massachusetts, from which part of his nickname derived, Rocky Marciano (his real name was Rocco Marchegiano) was heavyweight champion of the world from 1952 to 1956. Marciano won all of his 49 pro fights, 43 of which were knockout victories, including 11 KOs in the first round. The power of Marciano's punches and the devastating effect they had on opponents was the reason for the second half of his nickname. Marciano was killed in a light-plane crash in 1969 on the eve of his 46th birthday.

BRONCO NAGURSKI He came to the Chicago Bears in 1930 out of the University of Michigan, where he had been an All-American at both fullback and tackle. He went on to become one of the storied power runners in National Football League history. In the years 1933–37, plus 1943, Bronislaw Nagurski led the league in yards rushing. His nickname came from his habit of running with his head down, like a wild bucking bronco.

BRONX CHEER Another term for booing or razzing or raspberry, this sound allegedly originated in the Bronx in the 1920's. (The Bronx, one of the five boroughs of New York City, gets its name from the Dane Jonas Bronck, the man who first settled the area in 1641 for the Dutch West India Company.) The contemptuous sound sarcastically referred to as a "cheer" was made by vibrating the tongue between the lips.

BROOKLYN DODGER SYM-PHONY From 1938 to 1957

a group of unlikely musicians serenaded Dodger fans at Ebbets Field in Brooklyn. Sometimes they sat in seats 1–8, row 1, section 8. Sometimes they sauntered up and down the aisles, tooting and rooting on their beloved Bums. Sometimes they climbed up on top of the Dodger dugout and played their original form of jazz through the long summer days and nights. A special feature of the group was a tune they performed known as the "Army Duff." Fans referred to the song as "The Worms Crawl In." The little band would razz a visiting-team strikeout victim back to his bench with this song. As the player would sit down on his bench, the Sym-phony would accentuate the touch-down of his derrière with a blasting beat of the bass drum. There were many games of cat-and-mouse between the Sym-phony and strikeout victims who would feign seating themselves to avoid the last, razzing bass-drum beat. The Sym-phony always managed to time the touch-down and accentuate it musically to the delight of Dodger fans and to the dismay of the visiting players. Brooklyn broadcaster Red Barber originated the nickname for the group.

BROWN BOMBER This famous nickname for Joe Louis, heavyweight boxing champion of the world from 1937 to 1948, was derived from the color of his skin and the power of his punches. Louis won 68 of 71 fights—54 of them by knocking out his opponents.

BUCKHORSE This term is a British slang expression for a punch or a blow that became popular in 1850. Its origin lay in the actions of the famous English boxer John Smith, whose ring name was Buckhorse. For a few shillings, he would allow an individual to punch him on the side of the head as hard as possible. Ultimately, the blow became known as a buckhorse.

BUCKY Millions watched the 1978 World Series and saw the man they call Bucky Dent star in the field and at bat. The Yankee shortstop was voted the series Most Valuable Player award. But most people did not realize that "Bucky" was Dent's nickname. His real name is Russell Earl. The nickname Bucky was given to him by his grandmother—the word means a "small Indian boy."

BUGS RAYMOND Arthur Lawrence Raymond was a major-league pitcher for parts of six seasons in the early 1900's. He really had an apt nickname, as the following anecdote reveals. One day he was quietly eating his lunch in a restaurant. The waiter recognized him as a major league ball player and asked Bugs what the trick was in throwing the spitter. Bugs replied, "The whole thing is in the break." He then proceeded to demonstrate. Using a water glass for a baseball, he told the waiter to watch how his two fingers, which he had wet with water, gripped the glass. Then Bugs moved into his pitching motion, smilingly saying, "Watch the break." He threw the glass through a restaurant window and shouted, "See the break? That's how it's done."

BULL, THE Greg Luzinski was born the year of the "Whiz Kids," 1950, a time when a team of young Philadelphia Phillies amazed baseball by defeating the Brooklyn Dodgers and winning the National League pennant. Twenty years later, Luzinski became a member of the Philadelphia team. A 6'1", 220-pounder, his muscles and girth and power hitting have earned Greg his nickname.

BUMMY DAVIS Albert Abraham Davidoff was a Jewish boxer in the 1930's and 1940's. The popular explanation for his nickname is that he earned it as a result of the rough-and-tumble tactics he used as a boxer. Another and more interesting explanation is the Americanization of his Yiddish name, which went through stages from the original "Ahvroom" to "Boomy" and then "Bummy." Davis suffered a violent death. He attempted to break up a holdup in a Brooklyn bar. Fighting with the holdup man, Davis broke the man's jaw in two places. The holdup man then shot Bummy in the throat. Though mortally wounded, Davis still managed to chase the gunman into the street. But the gunman got away and Davis died of his wounds.

BUM OF THE MONTH CLUB In 1941 Joe Louis fought six bouts in six months, defeating all challengers. His victims were referred to as not-so-exclusive members of the Bum of the Month Club, a disparaging comment on their skills and the easy wins Louis had over them. Actually Louis did not seek out easy bouts. In his rule as heavyweight champ of the world—11 years, eight months, and 12 days (the longest reign of any heavyweight king)—the Brown Bomber risked his title 25 times and fought more often than any other champ.

BUMS, DEM When the Dodgers left Brooklyn in 1957, they left the "bums" behind. A beloved nickname in Flatbush, Gowanus, Bensonhurst, and Williamsburg, "Bums" was deemed not quite appropriate for the

Dodgers of Los Angeles. The nickname originated during the Depression. There was an excitable Brooklyn fan who used to scratch and claw at the chickenwire screen behind home plate at Ebbets Field. One day he was moved to anger at what he perceived as the inadequacies of the home team. "Ya, bum, ya, yez, bums, yez!" he bellowed. From that moment on, "Bums" meant Brooklyn Dodgers. The term was pictorialized by such cartoonists as Willard Mullin, used in newspaper headlines and stories, and capitalized on by the Dodger organization in its image-making for the Brooklyn team.

BUSBY BABES The Manchester United football (soccer) team of the late 1950's was very young and was managed by Matt Busby, and these facts earned it its nickname. In 1958, eight members of the team were killed when the plane carrying the "Busby Babes" crashed on takeoff from the airport in Munich. Four of those killed were also top members of the English national team. Bobby Charlton, who survived the crash, became one of the best of the European forwards.

BUTCH CASSIDY AND THE SUNDANCE KID The Dolphins of Miami went through an undefeated and untied 1972 NFL season, capping their winning ways with a Super Bowl triumph. The following year Miami lost only two games and recorded another Super Bowl triumph. Running backs Larry Csonka and Jim Kiick plowed out the yardage for the mighty Miami team and functioned as a potent team in their own right. Csonka, for example, notched a record 145 yards rushing in Super Bowl VIII. Their nickname came from the popular movie of the time about a pair of Western outlaws who were daringly efficient.

LADY BYNG MEMORIAL TROPHY The National Hockey League's award for best sportsmanship combined with a high standard of playing ability, the trophy originated in 1925 and was named for the wife of the then governor-general of Canada.

C

CADDIE The French had a hand in the insertion of this word into the language of sports. In 18th-century Scotland, a "caddie" (from the French word *cadet*) was a young fellow who ran around on errands or functioned as a porter. Eventually the young fellow and some older ones functioned as porters and ran around on errands looking for golf balls on courses, and they became known as caddies.

CALAMITY JANE Jane Burke was a Wild West character of song and story who was quick on the draw and noted for always prophesying calamities. She was nicknamed Calamity Jane. Golf great Bobby Jones had a putter characterized by a slightly lofted blade and a hickory shaft that had been broken in two places and bonded together again. Jones had great success with the putter he called Calamity Jane, especially in 1920 when it helped him win the British and American open and amateur championships.

CALDER MEMORIAL TROPHY The National Hockey League's trophy for a top rookie, it is named after former NHL President Frank Calder.

CANE PACE This one-mile stakes race for three-year-olds was named in honor of William H. Cane, former race-track president and respected improver of the breed. It is one of the races in pacing's Triple Crown.

CANNONBALL BAKER One of the legends of motorcycling is E. G. "Cannonball" Baker. He was the earliest of the transcontinental riders, coasting from Los Angeles to New York in eight days, 21 hours, and 16 minutes. That pioneer mark and most of the other speed and endurance records set by this man, who powered his machine as if it were a cannonball, have since been broken. Yet Baker remains in legend and in deed as perhaps the greatest at his craft that ever existed. He is best remembered for "cannonballing" back and forth between the coasts, setting and then breaking and then setting new records.

In 1935 he crossed the nation on his motorcycle for the 106th time. In 1941, the year of his final major run, then 60 years old, Baker made it across the country in six days, 6 hours, and 25 minutes—"And I didn't break any laws," he said.

"CAN'T ANYBODY HERE PLAY THIS GAME?" In 1960 Casey Stengel managed the New York Yankees to a first-place finish, on the strength of a .630 percentage compiled by winning 97 games and losing 57. By 1962 he was the manager of the New York Mets, a team that finished tenth in a ten-team league. They finished 60½ games out of first place, losing more games (120) than any other team in the 20th century. Richie Ashburn, who batted .306 for the Mets that season and then retired, remembers those days: "It was the only time I went to a ball park in the major leagues and nobody expected you to win."

A bumbling collection of castoffs, not-quite-ready-for-prime-time major league ball players, paycheck collectors, and callow youth, the Mets underwhelmed the opposition. They had Jay Hook, who could talk for hours about why a curve ball curved (he had a Masters degree in engineering) but couldn't throw one consistently. They had "Choo-Choo" Coleman, an excellent low-ball catcher, but the team had very few low-ball pitchers. They had "Marvelous Marv" Throneberry, a Mickey Mantle look-a-like in the batter's box—and that's where the resemblance ended. Stengel had been spoiled with the likes of Mantle, Maris, Ford, Berra, etc. Day after day he would watch the Mets and be amazed at how they could find newer and more original ways to beat themselves. In desperation—some declare it was on the day he witnessed pitcher Al Jackson go 15 innings yielding but three hits, only to lose the game on two errors committed by Marvelous Marv—Casey bellowed out his plaintive query, "Can't anybody here play this game?"

CARDIAC CARDINALS The St. Louis Cardinals of 1975 and 1976 were an explosive, exciting team. They had Terry Metcalf, Mel Gray, Jim Hart, and others capable of making the big play. Game after game, in the waning minutes—and sometimes seconds—of play, a long pass or a breakaway run would power the team to victory. They might be losing by a touchdown or more, but with their offensive tricks and skills they were never out of a game until the final gun sounded. The frequency and the drama of their comebacks caused heart palpitations among their rooters and earned the team its well-deserved nickname.

CARPETS In 1944 the National Football League witnessed the merger of the Pittsburgh Steelers and the Chicago Cardinals. The nickname for the merged team came from part of the name of each of the teams and was spelled and spoken as *carpet*. The team's record underscored its nickname, for every club in the league walked over it. The Carpets ended their one-year experimental merger with a record of no wins and ten losses.

"CASEY AT THE BAT" The title of the Ernest Thayer poem, written in 1888, about the legendary hero of the Mudville baseball team. The final stanzas are especially famous:

> The sneer is gone from Casey's lip; his teeth
> are clenched with hate;
> He pounds with cruel violence his bat upon
> the plate;
> And now the pitcher holds the ball, and now he
> lets it go,
> And now the air is shattered by the force of
> Casey's blow.

Oh, somewhere in this favored land, the sun
is shining bright;
The band is playing somewhere, and somewhere
hearts are light;
And somewhere men are laughing, and somewhere
children shout;
But there is no joy in Mudville—mighty Casey
has struck out!

CASH AND CARRY Charles C. Pyle was one of the
legendary promoters in sports. Dance marathons, six-
day bike races, tennis exhibitions, and the contracting
of Red Grange to play at $3,000 a game for the
Chicago Bears were among his accomplishments. Pyle
agreed with P. T. Barnum that "there's a sucker
born every minute." Pyle ran his business affairs with
money on an up-front basis, and that's how his nickname came about.

CATFISH HUNTER James Augustus Hunter is his real
name but the world knows him as Catfish, primarily
because of Oakland A's owner Charles O. Finley. Actually Hunter ran away from home when he was a child
and returned with two catfish. His parents called him
Catfish for a while and then the name was dropped.
Finley decided that Jim Hunter was too bland a name
for such a star pitcher. To add color and imagery,
Finley revived Hunter's childhood nickname and it has
stuck.

CHAIRMAN OF THE BOARD Whitey Ford pitched for the
New York Yankees for 16 seasons, winning 236
games, losing 106, and notching an earned-run average of 2.75. His .690 winning percentage places him

second on the all-time list. Ford knew how to win, knew how to take charge, knew how to preside over the Yankee fortunes—and all of these factors helped earn him his nickname.

CHARLEY HORSE There are a couple of legends as to how this term associated with the muscular cramps in the legs of athletes originated. Seventeenth-century English policemen—constables, or Charleys, as they were called—complained a good deal about leg and foot strain. The reference survived into 19th-century America. Ball players who complained about weary and tired legs claimed they were "riding Charley's horse." The other theory for the origin of the term points to an incident in the 1890's at the Chicago White Sox ball park, where a horse strained to pull a roller across the infield. The pulling was done stiffly by Charley the horse.

CHEVROLET The car was named after Louis Chevrolet, who designed the first model in 1911. Louis was the brother of Gaston, winner of the 1920 Indianapolis 500. The car Gaston Chevrolet drove was built by Louis. Both brothers, who were Frenchmen, were especially skilled racing drivers.

CHICOUTIMI CUCUMBER Georges Vezina, Montreal goalie (1917–26), was born in Chicoutimi, Quebec, in January 1887. Part of his nickname derived from his birthplace. The "cool as a cucumber" playing style used by Vezina explained the other half of his nickname. Overall, Vezina's nickname made for amusing alliteration and good sports copy, but it drove proofreaders wild (see VEZINA TROPHY).

CHIEF BENDER Charles Albert Bender won 210 games and compiled a 2.45 lifetime earned-run average in 16 years of pitching. He was admitted to baseball's Hall of Fame in 1953. His nickname came from the fact that he was a Chippewa Indian.

CHILDS CUP REGATTA This rowing race originated in 1879 and was named for the trophy donated by George W. Childs, publisher of the *Philadelphia Ledger*. It claims to be the second-oldest intercollegiate fixture. Originally it was a contest among Columbia, Princeton, and Pennsylvania universities. The regatta was suspended in 1884 but was resumed in 1912 as a competition between Pennsylvania and Princeton over a course of $1^5/_{16}$ miles at different venues.

CHINA WALL NHL goalie Johnny Bower played in an era when relations with Red China were not as open as they are today. His nickname stemmed from his ability to guard the net and allow few goals—just as the Great Wall of China allowed few outsiders to penetrate it.

CHOCTAW A graceful, fancy ice-skating step, this term is derived from the name of an Indian tribe of southern Mississippi. The Choctaws, one of the Five Civilized Tribes, got their name from the Spanish *chato* ("flattened"), because of the custom the Indians had of flattening the heads of male infants. How the actual skating maneuver—a half-turn from forward to backward or vice versa and a switch from one leg to the other that takes in a change of edge—is in reality related to the name of the Indian tribe is a matter of speculation.

CHOO-CHOO COLEMAN A catcher for the New York Mets during their early struggling years, Coleman is a case in point of the fact that not all things can be traced back to their origins. Once during a television interview, Coleman was asked how he got his nickname. He responded, "I don't know." He followed this up some time later with another gem. Casey Stengel, a bit frustrated by the ineptitude of the Mets, decided to return to basics. He held up a baseball during a locker-room meeting and said, "This is a baseball." Coleman interrupted, "Wait, you're going too fast."

CLOWN PRINCE OF BASEBALL Al Schacht performed for only three seasons as a member of the Washington Senators (1919–21), but he still was able to make a mighty reputation on the baseball field. Schacht was a comic and his routines centered on the foibles and eccentricities of the National Pastime. It was said that nobody did it better, and that's why Schacht was dubbed the Clown Prince.

CLYDE During the late 1960's and early 1970's Walt Frazier of the New York Knickerbockers of the National Basketball Association epitomized the cool, calculated precision of a daring basketball player. During his prime, the movie *Bonnie and Clyde,* about a bank-robbing duo, was popular. Frazier's facial hair, his elegant dress off the basketball court, his flashy car and mod ways, earned for him the nickname Clyde. He would steal the basketball, pass brilliantly, perform best under pressure, display an unruffled manner—all of which were the sporting counterparts to the characteristics of the movie antihero Clyde.

CODEBALL A physician, Dr. William E. Code, originated the sport that bears his name in the late 1920's. There

is "codeball-in-the-court," an outdoor game; and there
is "codeball-on-the-green," an indoor game. There is a
great deal of difference between the two sports, but the
ball they use is the same: it is six inches in diameter,
with a weight of 12 ounces.

COMMERCE COMET Mickey Mantle burst onto the
major league baseball scene with the New York Yankees in 1951 and called it a career after 18 storied
seasons. Four times he led the American League in
home runs. He was a rare blend of raw power and
blinding speed—tape-measure home runs and track-
star dashes down the baseline to first. He came from
Commerce, Oklahoma, and lit up major league
baseball.

COURT TENNIS This sport has a lavish and majestic history. Its name comes from the royal courts and the
members of those courts who played the game. A
Frenchman, Peter Garnier, is credited with originating
the sport that so impressed Phillipe Le Bel that in order
to have a court available at all times, he purchased a
hotel in 1308. As the years passed, royalty outdid one
another in designing and decorating magnificent courts
for the playing of what they referred to as royal tennis.

CRAB, THE The middle man in the famed Tinker to Evers
to Chance double-play combination, Johnny Evers was
a pugnacious and combative ball player and manager.
Admitted to the Hall of Fame in 1946, Evers had an
18-year playing career and managed for three other
years. His ingoing personality and bench-jockeying
ability gave him his nickname on merit.

CRAZY LEGS A star (1949–57) for the Los Angeles

Rams, Elroy Hirsch had a career that saw him go from success to tragedy and back to success again. So poignant and melodramatic was his life that Hollywood even made a movie based on it, *Crazy Legs: All American*. He was just grooving into a successful career in 1948 when he suffered a fractured skull in a collision on the football field. There was a temporary loss of body coordination, and doctors told him he would never be able to play again. They were wrong. He went on to become pro football's first flanker and helped revolutionize the sport. His nickname came from the wild and almost uncontrolled way his legs splayed behind him when he ran, from his full-out running—head back, arms stretched out to grasp a flying football on his fingertips, legs churning out yardage and leaving defenders behind.

CRICKET Cricket gets its name from the Anglo-Saxon word *cryce,* a term used to describe a wooden stick used to hit a ball. The earliest recorded cricket match took place in 1697.

CROQUET Around 1300 the French played a game called *Paile-Maille,* which was the grandfather of croquet. The French word *croche,* a reference to a crooked stick, is the origin of the name for the sport of croquet. Most people associate the sport with England because of its 19th-century popularity on wide English lawns perfectly suited for the playing of the game.

CROW, THE A fairly little man with a screechy voice, Frank Crosetti fit his nickname. He played shortstop for the New York Yankees for 17 years and then had a long stint as a coach with the team.

CURTIS CUP British sisters Harriot and Margaret Curtis were excellent golfers who between them won the United States Ladies Golf Championship four times. In 1932 they presented the Curtis Cup for competition. Teams of women golfers representing each country compete for the cup annually, with the site alternating between Great Britain and the United States.

CY THE SECOND Irving Melrose Young pitched for six years in the major leagues concurrently with Denton True Young—the storied "Cy" Young who won 508 games in his career. Irving Young only won 62, while losing 94, but the fact that he had the same last name and pitched at the same time as the great Cy Young earned Irving his nickname (see CY YOUNG AWARD).

CY THE THIRD In 1908, a year in which Cy Young won 21 games and compiled a 1.26 earned-run average, Harley E. Young made it to the major leagues. He pitched only 75⅔ innings, losing three games and winning none. But because his last name and the time he played reminded fans of the great Cy Young, Harley was called Cy the Third (see CY YOUNG AWARD).

D

DAFFINESS BOYS Also known as Dem Brooklyn Bums, the 1926 Brooklyn Dodgers wrought havoc on friend and foe alike. The hotshot of the team was free-swinging, slump-shouldered Babe Herman, dubbed the Incredible Hoiman, who bragged that among his stupendous feats was stealing second base with the bases loaded. Once Herman was one of a troika of Dodger baserunners who found themselves all on third base at the same time. A Dodger rookie turned to Brooklyn manager "Uncle" Wilbert Robinson on the bench. "You call that playing baseball?" "Uncle" Robbie responded, "Leave them alone. That's the first time they've been together all year."

DAN PATCH The only world-champion harness-racing horse never to have lost a race, this legendary horse set a record in 1905 for pacing the mile that stood until 1938. During his career the name Dan Patch became synonymous with "racehorse" and people came out in record numbers just to catch a glimpse of him en route to and from tracks. He earned more than $3 million for his owners. There was Dan Patch chewing-tobacco. There were Dan Patch cigars. There were Dan Patch pillows. There were Dan Patch washing-machines. People even danced the Dan Patch two-step. At the time of his retirement, in 1909, Dan Patch held nine world records. He died on July 11, 1916, and the next day his owner, Marion Willis Savage, died, too. Heart ailments were the cause of death for both horse and owner.

DAVIS CUP In 1900 Dwight Filley Davis (1879–1945) donated a silver cup designed to be awarded as a national trophy to the country triumphing in an international competition in lawn tennis. The donation took place while Davis was still an undergraduate at Harvard. From the start, all teams consisted of four amateur players. All Davis Cup contests include four singles matches and one doubles match. Davis was one of the more outstanding tennis players in United States history, as well as a high-ranking government official in the 1920's and 1930's.

DAZZY VANCE A pitcher with mediocre Brooklyn Dodger teams for most of his 16 years, the Dazzler, as he was also known, did not publicize his full name— Clarence Arthur Vance. His nickname came from the blazing speed he put on his fastball. His big windup and dazzling fastball enabled him to lead the National

League in strikeouts seven straight years. Vance, who recorded his first major league victory at the age of 31, was characterized by former New York Giant great George "Highpockets" Kelly as follows: "Heck, you knew what he was going to throw—the dazzler—and you still couldn't hit him." At the age of 37, in 1928, he won 22 games and was the league ERA leader with a sixth-place team. That wasn't his best year. In 1924 the Hall of Famer put together a 28-6 record, 262 strikeouts, and a 2.16 earned-run average to really dazzle National League hitters.

HENRI DELAUNAY CUP This trophy, originated in 1960, serves as the symbol of victory in the European Nations Cup, a soccer competition staged on the same elimination system as the World Cup and held every four years between the cycle of the World Cup. Henri Delaunay was a leading personality in French soccer and one of those instrumental in helping to create the World Cup.

DERBY (ENGLISH) The American name for a version of the felt, dome-shaped hat that the English call a bowler, the *derby* gets its name from the twelfth earl of Derby, Edward Stanley (d. 1834), who came from a family that traced its roots back to William the Conqueror. The Earl was an avid supporter of horse racing and spent most of his time improving the breed and, allegedly, ignoring his wife. In 1780 he inaugurated a series of annual races for three-year-olds at Epsom Downs, a track at which races had been held for quite a while. The race suggested by the Earl was named in his honor—the English Derby.

DIT CLAPPER National Hockey League Hall of Famer Audrey Victor Clapper was always better known by his nickname, Dit. For 20 years he wore the number 5 on the back of his Boston Bruins uniform. He explained his nickname this way: "When I was a child, my parents called me Vic. I couldn't said *Vic*. I'd lisp the name, and it came out *Dit*. The name stuck, sort of."

DIVOT Golfers become part-time gardeners as they replace the piece of sod ripped out by their clubs. The piece of sod is referred to as a *divot,* which is a Scottish word meaning a piece of turf.

DIZZY and DAFFY DEAN Perhaps the most famous of all brother acts in the history of sports was "Me and Paul," the dazzling Dean brothers of the St. Louis Cardinals. Jerome Hannah Dean, also known as Jay Hannah Dean and best known as Dizzy, and his kid brother Paul, also known as Daffy, beguiled National League batters in the 1930's and at times drove their own teammates to despair with their madcap antics.

The brothers were born in a rickety shack on a plot of Arkansas ground that their destitute sharecropper parents worked. Dizzy picked cotton for 50 cents a day, and although he later bragged that he learned how to pitch while attending Oklahoma State Teachers College, he only went as far as the second grade in school. In Dizzy, and to a lesser extent Paul, was the sadness and brashness of the American Depression experience. "Some of the things I seen in this here life," Dizzy recalled, "almost cause my ol' heart to bust right through my sweatshirt."

Dizzy grew to be a 6'2", slope-shouldered right-hander, a little bigger than his younger brother. Both of them had arms and hands toughened and shaped by the cotton fields. "I never bothered what those guys could hit and couldn't hit," he said. "All I knowed is that they weren't gonna get a-holt of that ball ol' Diz was throwin'."

In 1934, Dizzy and Daffy won 49 games between them. Dizzy won 30—more than any Cardinal pitcher ever. In a doubleheader against Brooklyn, Diz one-hit the Dodgers in the first game and Paul no-hit them in the second game. "If I'd a knowed Paul was gonna do that," Diz said, "I'd a done the same."

Dizzy was actually the zanier brother. Paul went along with his antics and thus was labeled Daffy. Dizzy once wrapped himself in a blanket and made a fire in front of the Cardinal dugout on a day when the temperature was over 100 degrees. Dizzy once led Daffy and a couple of other Cardinals into a staid hotel and announced to the manager that he was under orders to redecorate the place. Armed with ladders, buckets of paint, and brushes, the baseball players proceeded to splash red paint with wild abandon all over the walls of the hotel lobby. Dizzy also once made more than a mild commotion when he told scouts and newspapermen that there was a third Dean "who was throwin' real good at Tulsa." When the tip was checked out, it turned out that the third Dean brother who was "throwing real good" was throwing bags of peanuts—he was a peanut vendor at the Tulsa ball park.

The Deans had bright but relatively brief careers.

Paul won 19 games in both 1934 and 1935 and then lapsed into a journeyman pitcher role, the victim of arm trouble. In the 1937 All-Star Game, Dizzy had a line shot off the bat of Earl Averill carom off his right foot. They found out later that his toe was broken. Diz pitched again and again during the 1937 season, but he was not what he was; the fluid, cottonpicking pitching motion was gone. He finished the year with a 13–10 record, and in 1938 he was sent to the Cubs for two pitchers and $200,000. He won seven, lost one, and had an ERA of 1.81, but that was his last year of pitching effectiveness. They were Dizzy and Daffy, but in their time they beguiled baseball fans and intimidated National League hitters.

DR. J. Agile and talented Julius Erving, one of the premier stars first of the American Basketball Association and now of the National Basketball Association, can do tricks with a basketball. Neither his first nor his last name conjures up images of a driving, talented, cool basketball player. Thus, the "Dr." stems from what he can do with a basketball and an ailing team, and the "J" is a more relevant-sounding abbreviation for his first name.

DODGERS The early years of the Brooklyn National League baseball team saw it called by many different nicknames. They were called Brooklyns and Brooks. At one point in their history, quite a few of the players happened to get married at about the same time, and "Bridegrooms" became the new nickname. They were also called Superbas, after a famed vaudeville act, and Robins, in tribute to the manager of that era, Wilbert

Robinson. The borough of Brooklyn circa 1900 was an area linked by trolleys. To Manhattan residents, it appeared that the citizens of Brooklyn were always dodging these trolleys. The contemptuous reference to those living in Brooklyn was the term *trolley dodgers*. Eventually, since the area where the Brooklyn team played was near a web of trolley tracks, the team was called the Trolley Dodgers. This was ultimately shortened to "Dodgers." Even in 1958, when Walter O'Malley moved the team to Los Angeles, he was able to leave Brooklyn behind but the "Dodgers" went along.

DOGGETT'S COAT AND BADGE In his will, English actor Thomas Doggett made provisions for the awarding of a trophy to the winner of a race of approximately 4½ miles on the Thames River between London Bridge and Chelsea. The race was first held in 1715, and its prize has been awarded annually to the winning crew of novice oarsmen. It is the oldest continuously-granted trophy in the world of sports. The trophy is actually an orange-colored livery (coat) and a badge that represents Liberty. The "coat," the "badge," and Doggett's name are combined in the title of the trophy.

DOLLAR BILL His contract with the New York Knickerbockers called for $500,000 for four years' work, but the nickname given Bill Bradley was not for the money he earned but for the money he saved. While other NBA stars drove flashy cars and sported ever more lavish wardrobes, Bradley lived simply and dressed even more simply. His apartment, one friend said, "looked like a Holiday Inn room before the maid shows up." Bradley reportedly used paper clips when his cuff buttons gave out. There was a precedent for his behavior. While a Rhodes Scholar at Oxford for two years, Bradley lived out of what was called "a large and appallingly messy suitcase"; he had more important things on his mind than style and consumer comforts. His nickname was a taunting reference to the fact that many players thought he still owned the first buck he ever made.

"DON'T LOOK BACK. SOMETHING MIGHT BE GAINING ON YOU" This line of homespun wisdom formed the sixth rule of a recipe attributed to former baseball pitching great Leroy "Satchel" Paige. The other five rules were (1) avoid fried meats which angry up the blood; (2) if your stomach disputes you, lie down and pacify it with cool thoughts; (3) keep your juices flowing by jangling around gently as you move; (4) go very gently on the vices, such as carrying on in society—the social ramble ain't restful; (5) avoid running at all times. It seems that most of us have managed to break all of Mr. Paige's rules more than once. As for rule 5—don't tell it to your neighborhood jogger.

DORMIE In golf, a player is in this condition if he is as many holes up as there are holes remaining to be played. Apparently the term evolved from the French word *endormi* ("asleep"). Thus, a player who is dormie up "can go to sleep," for there is not much purpose for further exertion.

DOUBLE X Hall of Famer Jimmie Foxx had two nicknames. His main one was derived from the last two letters of his name. He was also known as the Beast, which indicated the way his rivals viewed his baseball-playing ability. Foxx averaged better than a hit a game in a 20-year career, compiling a .325 batting average and a .609 slugging percentage. He hit 534 homers, scored over 1,700 runs and drove in almost 2,000 runs.

DUCKPIN BOWLING The sport and its name were both invented in 1900 through the efforts of baseball Hall of Famers John J. McGraw and Wilbert Robinson. At the time both men were partners in the Diamond Bowling Alleys in Baltimore. Seeking a variation on the bowling game, they had the ten-pins transformed into smaller pins in conformity with the six-inch ball used for bowling in a game of that time called 5-back or cocked hat. When they watched their first set of little pins fly helter-skelter, the baseball immortals, both expert duck-shooters, claimed it looked as if the pins were a flock of flying ducks. It was actually Bill Clarke, a Baltimore sportswriter, who stuck the label *duck pins* on the new pins and the new game. Clarke allegedly coined the term after the comments of McGraw and Robinson.

DUKE, THE There have been many athletes dubbed Duke, but Edwin Donald "Duke" Snider, the man also known as the Silver Fox because of the color of his hair, has a lock on the nickname. From 1947 to 1957 he starred in center field for the old Brooklyn Dodgers. Although the New York Giants had Willie Mays and the New York Yankees had Joe DiMaggio and then Mickey Mantle playing the same position, to Brooklyn fans Snider was the Duke—their royalty. He fit the name well. A handsome, tempestuous left-handed slugger, Snider was a vital part of the Dodger machine. "Somebody once asked me if I wanted to be 25 years old again," he said. "Not if I had to trade those Brooklyn Dodger days. It was something special."

DUMMY William Ellsworth Hoy, a major league baseball player in the years 1888–1902, was only five feet, four inches tall and weighed only 148 pounds. Yet his lifetime batting average was .288. His nickname was a little more than insensitive, for Bill Hoy was a deaf-mute.

DYNAMITE LINE Cooney Weiland, Dutch Gainor, and Dit Clapper powered the Boston Bruins to the 1929 National Hockey League championship. The explosive scoring and checking power of this line earned it its nickname (see DIT CLAPPER).

E

EARTHQUAKES The nickname of the San Jose team of the North American Soccer League is derived from the fact that the team plays its home games not too far from the San Andreas Fault.

EASY ED A lean 6′8″, 190-pounder, Ed Macauley ranks as one of the top centers in NBA history. A three-time All-Star in a nine-year playing career during the 1950's, Macauley specialized in a smooth, almost unstoppable hook shot and driving layups. His temperament and his performing skills were characterized by an ease and a grace that was reflected in his nickname.

EBBETS FIELD On April 9, 1913, the Brooklyn Dodgers played their first game in their new ball park against the Philadelphia Phillies. An account of the event read: "A cold, raw wind kept the attendance down to about

12,000, but did not affect the players, who put up a remarkable battle. Both Tom Seaton (Philadelphia) and Nap Rucker (Brooklyn) pitched brilliant ball, the former just shading the noted southpaw in a 1 to 0 shutout. The opening ceremonies were impressive, the two teams parading across the field headed by a band. . . . Casey Stengel made a sensational catch. . . . ''

The site of the ball park was four-and-a-half acres on the lower slope of Crown Heights in Brooklyn, a filled-in tract of marshy land that the neighborhood people called Pigtown. Ebbets Field originally seated 18,000, with another 3,000 standees able to watch the games. The park had a double-decked grandstand that extended around the right-field foul line virtually to the fence in left field. A small, open bleacher section with concrete seats was located in left between the stands and the field. Beyond right field was Bedford Avenue. It was a confined, intimate, tiny, odd-shaped ball park—and it was a place that on the day it opened became obsolete and needed architectural and seating changes. The man the park was named for was Charles H. Ebbets, who moved from selling peanuts and scorecards to the presidency and primary ownership of the Brooklyn National League franchise. It was his vision that created the fabled ball park.

EEPHUS BALL A specialty of Pittsburgh Pirate pitcher Truett "Rip" Sewell, this pitch sort of sailed to the plate in a high, lazy arc that tantalized overeager hitters. With his trick pitch, Sewell won 42 games in 1943 and 1944.

EIGHTH WONDER OF THE WORLD On what was once

Texas swampland and a wind-swept prairie, the Houston Astros play baseball in the Astrodome, which many have nicknamed the Eighth Wonder of the World. Built at a cost of $38 million, the colossal complex sprawls over 260 acres six miles from downtown Houston. The facility has the biggest electric scoreboard and the largest dome ever constructed. It is the largest clear-span building ever built and it is the largest air-conditioned stadium ever. The Astrodome has 45,000 plush opera-type seats, from which fans can view athletic events in the aditional comfort supplied by a 6,000-ton air-conditioning system that maintains the temperature in the stadium at 72 degrees. The inspiration for the Astrodome was the Roman Colosseum, built circa 80 A.D., which prodded Judge Roy Hofheinz, president of the Houston Sports Association, the owners of the team, to press for the creation of a domed stadium. "I knew with our heat, humidity and rain, the best chance for success was in the direction of a weather-proof, all-purpose stadium," said Hofheinz. Buckminster Fuller, media-famed ecologist and inventor of the geodesic dome, served as consultant to the project. Hofheinz said, "Buckminster Fuller convinced me that it was possible to cover any size space so long as you didn't run out of money." They didn't run out of money and even had $2 million to spare for the 300-ton scoreboard, with 1,200 feet of wiring, that stretches 474 feet across the brown pavilion seats in center field.

EISENHOWER CUP Named for former president Dwight D. Eisenhower, who presented it, this cup originated in 1958. It symbolizes a golf tournament for teams of four amateurs from each competing country. It is also known as the World Cup.

$11,000 LEMON In 1908 Rube Marquard was purchased by John McGraw of the New York Giants from the minor league Indianapolis team. The $11,000 paid for Marquard was a record sum paid for a minor leaguer at that time. Since Marquard's record during his first three years with the Giants was nine wins and 18 losses, McGraw's judgment was criticized and Marquard was labeled the "$11,000 Lemon." However, in 1911 the left-handed pitcher rewarded McGraw's patience and showed that the Giant manager's judgment was correct by achieving a record of 24–7. The next year his record 19 consecutive victories powered the Giants to the National League pennant. And there were those who then called him the "$11,000 Wonder."

ENGLISH This term, denoting spin, twist, or movement on a baseball, tennis ball, or billard ball, was probably derived from *body English*—all those hand, shoulder, and posture moves used when words are not sufficient to describe something as accurately and as colorfully as possible. The popular theory that the word as used in sports is derived from the off-beat or tricky ways of Englishmen is just a case—or so the story goes—of Americans getting back at the Mother Country one more time.

EPSOM DOWNS Located within the circle at the Epsom racetrack in Surrey, this is an area where the gypsy caravans mingle for the four-day English race meeting in June. Free admission makes the area especially crowded on Derby day.

ERA This term is both the initials of the English Racing

Association and the name given in 1934 to a series of racing cars designed by Peter Berthon.

ERASER, THE HUMAN Marvin Webster of the New York Knickerbockers in the National Basketball Association earned his nickname for his shot-blocking ability. At seven-feet-plus, Webster's size and timing has enabled him to wipe out scoring efforts of opponents by simply batting the ball away from the hoop.

F

FASTNET, THE This major offshore race is sailed in August of every other year (alternating with the New York-to-Bermuda race) over a distance of 605 miles, from Cowes, Isle of Wight, to the Fastnet Rock (off Cape Clear, in southwest Ireland), and back to Plymouth. The race originated in 1925. The name of the race is derived from Fastnet Rock.

FATHER OF AMERICAN FOOTBALL Walter Camp introduced and pushed through many changes in the game of football that modernized the sport, and that earned him his nickname. Yale team captain from 1876 to 1881, Camp was a key member of the Intercollegiate Football Association rules committee from 1878 to 1925. It was he who convinced that important committee to cut a football playing squad from 15 to

11 players and to delegate a center to hike the ball to another player who called the signals, thus creating the scrimmage. Camp also had a hand in other changes that laid the foundations of the game of football as we know it today.

FATTY One of the broadest fellows ever to take up space on a soccer field was William J. Foulke, an English goal tender. He played in the years 1874–1916. Foulke stood 6'3" and weighed 311 pounds. He covered up a large part of the goal just by being there. Mr. Foulke once interrupted the progress of a game by jumping and then leaning too heavily on the crossbar, snapping it.

FENWAY PARK The Boston Red Sox moved into their new home in 1912 on the property of the Fenway Realty Company at Landsdowne and Jersey streets. Although it was rebuilt in 1934, it is essentially the way it was at the time of its birth. Its "Green Monster"—the 37-foot-high wall extending from the foul pole in left field 315 feet from home plate to the flagpole 388 feet from home well past left-center—is its most distinctive feature. The park's seating capacity is only 33,379, which makes every seat in the house excellent for close-up viewing.

FIRST TELEVISED SPORTS EVENT On May 17, 1939, over station W2XBS, a 16-man NBC crew with equipment costing $100,000 sent out the first televised sports coverage. The subject was the Princeton-Columbia baseball game from Baker Field in New York. A single camera was used, and the total cost of transmittal was $3,000. There were no close-ups of

action. The players on the television screen looked like
white flies. The single camera was stationed near the
third-base line, and it swept back and forth across the
diamond. Instant replay, "slo-mo," split screen,
Zoomar lens, hand-held cameras, instant isolates,
overhead blimps, graphics, Monday Night Football,
and Super Bowl were not even dimly perceived by the
average fan, but on June 5, 1939, an editorialist for
Life magazine showed some vision:

No fuzziness (in the telecast) could hide what
television will mean for American sports. . . .
Within ten years an audience of 10,000,000 sit-
ting at home or in the movie theaters will see the
World Series or the Rose Bowl game. . . .
Thousands of men and women who have never
seen a big-time sports event will watch the moving shadows on the television screen and become
excited fans. . . ."

BILLY FISKE MEMORIAL TROPHY The most desired
trophy in bobsledding, it is named for one of the most
famous American competitors in the sport. Fiske enlisted in the Royal Air Force in 1939, when World War
II began. He died from wounds he suffered while
flying a mission. The award in his name is for the
National AAU four-man competition. Fiske is remembered for his driving a five-man U.S. team to triumph
in the 1928 Winter Olympic Games and then repeating
this feat four years later at Lake Placid, N.Y.

FLYING DUTCHMAN Honus Wagner played for the
Pittsburgh Pirates for 21 years, winning eight batting
titles, collecting 3,430 hits, and establishing team rec-

ords for most doubles, triples, and extra-base hits. He
played every position except catcher, but he earned his
fame as a shortstop. Of Dutch origin, he was a speedy
base runner, leading the National League five times in
stolen bases and recording a career total of 722 stolen
bases. His speed and his Dutch heritage blended together to form his nickname, the Flying Dutchman.

FORE This traditional shout to other golfers or bystanders
to caution them that they may be hit by a ball is apparently an abridged version of the cry "Beware before."

FOSBURY FLOP Dick Fosbury in the mid-1960's attracted
national attention for his unorthodox technique in the
high jump. The technique, in which the jumper goes
over the bar head first and backwards, was good
enough to earn Fosbury a gold medal in the 1968
Olympics in Mexico City.

FOUR HORSEMEN "Outlined against a blue-gray October
sky, the Four Horsemen rode again. In dramatic lore
they are known as Famine, Pestilence, Destruction and
Death. These are only aliases. Their real names are
Stuhldreher, Miller, Crowley and Layden. . . ." Those
lines from a column written by Grantland Rice in the
New York *Herald-Tribune* opened his description of
how Notre Dame's football team defeated Army,
13–7 in 1924. His romantic reference has become the
very personification of the power and mystique of football in America.

FOUR MUSKETEERS English-speaking nations domi-
nated the first 26 years of the Davis Cup tennis competition. In 1927 France broke through as a result of the
efforts of René Lacoste, Henri Cochet, Jean Bototra,

and Jacques Brugnon. The four Frenchmen were dubbed the Four Musketeers, and they were responsible for keeping the Davis Cup in France for six straight years.

FRANCHISE, THE An often-used term that describes an athlete whose value to an organization transcends his or her value on the playing field. The two most recent famous "franchises" have been Lou Brock and Tom Seaver. Brock's record-breaking feats with the St. Louis Cardinals and his base-stealing skills not only enabled his team to win but also to attract fans, swelling the attendance. Seaver, as a New York Met, anchored the pitching staff and added to the image of the team. When he pitched, attendance would also increase many times, for there were those who were Seaver fans more than they were fans of the Mets.

*Bill Bradley (Dollar Bill),
before the days of the
Senate, when he earned his
salary dribbling the ball for
the New York Knicker-
bockers*

*A great matchup—Clyde
versus Dr. J.—Walt Frazier,
#10, guarded by Julius
Erving, #6*

*The Mahatma and the Lip—Branch Rickey and Leo Durocher
in conference in Brooklyn Dodger office. Durocher had just
been reinstated as manager in 1948.*

*Broadway Joe Namath in full New
York Jet football gear, poised for
passing*

Muhammad Ali of "Rope-A-Dope" fame—as fast with his lips as he was with his fists

The legendary Satchel Paige, who never looked back—looking ahead to a major league career with the Cleveland Indians in 1948 as a 42-year-old (?) rookie

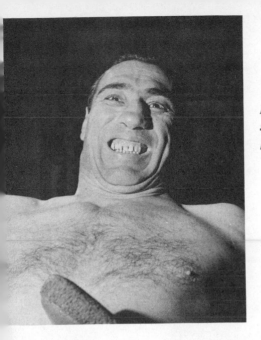

Primo Carnera (The Ambling Alp) showing off his hairy chest and pearly teeth

BELOW: *Golfer Arnold Palmer in a typical walk down the fairway, with his "army" tagging along*

The first black heavyweight champion—Jack Johnson flashing power and style

The Rose Bowl in Pasadena, California—filled to capacity

Jim Thorpe, one of America's greatest all-time, all-around athletes, in just one of the many uniforms he wore

The Yankee Clipper (Joe DiMaggio), circa 1944 in a different uniform

Golf's Curtis Cup inscribed with the names of its donors, Harriot and Margaret Curtis

Rodeo action north of the border

A very young Red Barber doing what he did best—broadcasting
Brooklyn Dodger baseball from Ebbets Field

The "old perfessor," Casey Stengel, with a left-handed Met hopeful
and Hall of Famer Warren Spahn looking on

ABOVE: *Clown Prince of Baseball Al Schacht with one of the routines that made him famous*

RIGHT: *The sledge-hammer-like power of karate, cracking wide open a two-pound brick from top to bottom*

The Grand Prix event—July 10, 1947 in Lausanne, Switzerland. Car #4 on the right driven by Villoresi of Italy, the winner

A clean-shaven "Barber"—Sal Maglie being kissed by his wife before the 1951 Brooklyn Dodger–New York Giant National League play-off— "Dat Day"

G

GALLOPING GHOST An All-American at the University of Illinois three straight years in the early 1920's, Harold "Red" Grange scored 31 touchdowns and gained 3,637 yards. His running skills and evasive techniques were so potent that he was able almost to "disappear" from opponents, and that's how his nickname came to be. Grange was also known as the Flying Terror in tribute to what he could do to the opposition. After signing with the Chicago Bears in 1925, Grange became such an attraction that some observers credit him with almost singlehandedly establishing professional football.

GARRISON FINISH The name of the winning rider in the 1882 Suburban horse race, Edward H. ("Snapper") Garrison, has become identified in all sports and in other areas of life with coming on strong down the homestretch and winning. Snapper Garrison held back his mount, Montana, until the very last moment in that 1882 Suburban. Garrison then stood high in the stirrups and crouched very low over the horse's mane, in what became famous as the "Yankee seat." He whipped Montana, and the horse streaked ahead of the other horses to win the race by a nose. The Garrison technique, used over and over again throughout the jockey's long and successful career, consisted of coming from behind to win a race with a stretch run in the last furlong.

GARRYOWN The roots for this term, which describes a high-lofted kick in rugby, come from the Irish rugby club of the same name. Employed as an offensive maneuver, this punt is used to gain ground, especially in those situations when forwards surge down the field.

GASHOUSE GANG The St. Louis Cardinals of the mid-1930's earned this nickname because of their unique individual personalities and their spirited performances on and off the field. Mingled together to make baseball history were such competitors as "the Dazzling Deans," Dizzy and his brother Paul; Pepper Martin, who as a third baseman used his chest to stop ground balls; Joe "Ducky" Medwick, also known as the Hungarian Rhapsody because of his verve and drive and Hungarian origins; and a young shortstop named Leo Durocher, who some were already calling Screechy because of his nonstop chatter. On the field they played with wild abandon—stealing bases, taking chances, fighting with each other and the opposition, covering their uniforms with dirt so that it "appeared as if they worked in a gashouse and not a ball park," as one observer declared. And that was how the nickname was born.

In the 1934 World Series, Joe Medwick did more than astonish thousands and thousands of Detroit Tiger fans. The Cardinals were on their way to a seventh-game 11–0 romp over Detroit. In the sixth inning of that game, Medwick tripled and allegedly spiked Tiger third baseman Marv Owen. Taking his left-field position the next inning, Medwick was bombarded with rotten fruit, beer bottles, raw eggs, and other missiles. Ducky did not duck, but stuck out his jaw and called for more. Baseball Commissioner Landis called for Medwick and informed him that he was taking him out of the game for the good of baseball—and for the good of Medwick. The Gashousers earned their name for many things, but this was the first time one of them, one wit observed, was removed from a game because he smelled up the playing field (see DIZZY and DAFFY DEAN, and WILD HORSE OF THE OS-AGE).

GENTLEMAN JIM   The first of the modern world heavyweight champs, James J. Corbett defeated John L. Sullivan on September 7, 1892. It was the first match staged in the United States under Queensberry rules and with five-ounce gloves. The bout ended in the 21st round, when Corbett kayoed Sullivan, culminating a fight that pitted a scientific boxer against a slugger. Sullivan retired after the defeat. Corbett's nickname had its roots in his stylized manner of dress, his pompadour hair comb, and his intelligent, articulate, mannered behavior (see QUEENSBERRY RULES).

GEORGIA PEACH Tyrus Raymond Cobb, baseball immortal, played 22 seasons for the Detroit Tigers and two more for the Philadelphia Athletics. He also managed Detroit in the years 1921–26. Cobb compiled a lifetime batting average of .367, stole 892 bases, and won 12 batting titles in a span of 13 years. By the time he retired, he had set 90 individual records. Cobb was born in Narrows, Georgia, and his nickname was partially derived from his native state, which is called the Peach State. His nickname is also rooted in the glorious but tempestuous talent of the man many claim to be the greatest baseball player of all time. Cobb was not one who fit the stereotype of the typical Southern gentleman. Once he almost demolished a baseball roommate as they jostled to get to the bathroom. "I just had to be first," was Cobb's response—and his way of life.

GERTIE George Gravel was a National Hockey League official in the late 1940's. His unusual nickname was inspired by the Dick Tracy comic-strip character Gravel Gertie.

"GETTING A TIE IS LIKE KISSING YOUR SISTER" For Vince Lombardi of the Green Bay Packers, winning wasn't the only thing—it was the enjoying of winning that also counted. A driven, dedicated coach, Lombardi hated finishing second. There were times during his career when his teams could have played it safe and settled for a tie rather than risk defeat. Lombardi's passion for victory and his apathy toward "no decision" is reflected in the above quote.

GIANTS One sultry summer's day in 1885, Jim Mutrie, the

saber-mustached manager of the New York Gothams, was enjoying himself watching his team winning an important game. Mutrie screamed out with affection, "My big fellows, my giants." Many of his players were big fellows, and they came to be Giants. For that was how the nickname Giants came to be. And when the New York team left for San Francisco in 1958, *Giants,* Mutrie's endearing nickname, went along with it.

GO-GO SOX The 1959 Chicago White Sox won the team's first American League pennant in 40 years, as they excited Windy City fans and others throughout the United States with their distinctive style of baseball. As a team, the Sox batted only .250, but their 113 stolen bases paced the majors and they parlayed speed and daring into a playing pattern good for 94 wins. Where there was an opportunity to take an extra base, the White Sox took it. Where there was a chance to use their speed or their bunting ability, they capitalized on it. Seemingly always on the move and using what ability they had to maximum advantage, the White Sox earned the nickname of Go-Go Sox, whose assets they inflicted on the opposition. Their siege gun was Luis Aparicio ("Little Looie"), a 5'9", 160-pound speedster who led the majors in stolen bases with 56. Aparicio also batted .332, walked 52 times, and scored 98 runs to pace the "go" in the Go-Go Sox.

"GOING, GOING, GONE" Originated by former New York Yankee broadcaster Mel Allen, this phrase has become part of the popular language. Allen used the words to describe the suspense generated by balls hit to

the distant reaches of Yankee Stadium, which traveled
and traveled until they went out of the playing field and
into home run territory. Sometimes just "Going, going" was uttered—as the ball would be caught before it
was "gone."

GOLDEN BEAR Famed golfer Jack Nicklaus earned this
nickname because of his size and hair color.

GOLDEN GLOVES When this competition originated in
1927 under the sponsorship of the New York *Daily
News*, it was strictly an amateur boxing competition
for fighters in the New York City area. Today the
competition is both national and international. Arch
Ward, former sports editor of the Chicago *Tribune,*
was mainly responsible for making the event international. He set up All-American and All-European title
fights. Many top fighters got their start in the Golden
Gloves: Sugar Ray Robinson, Joe Louis, Barney Ross,
Tony Zale, Rocky Marciano—all world champs at one
time or another.

GOLDEN GREEK Harry Agganis, of Greek ancestry, was
born on April 20, 1930, and died, too young, on June
27, 1955. A powerfully built player, Agganis batted
.251 his first year as a member of the Boston Red Sox,
and .313 in his second and final year. The unrealized
potential of Agganis makes his nickname especially
poignant.

GOLDEN HAWK Bobby Hull, ten-time National Hockey
League All-Star, seven-time NHL goal-scoring leader,
and three-time winner of the scoring championship,
had blond hair and starred for the Chicago Black
Hawks—and that's how his nickname came to be. Hull

has been called the fastest player on ice—he was
clocked at 29.7 miles per hour when in his prime.
After the 1971–72 season, Hull became player-coach
of the Winnipeg Jets of the World Hockey Association. A new league and a new team gave him a new
nickname—the Golden Jet. The "Jet" part of the
nickname was for his new team. The "Golden," some
said, was because of his ten-year contract totaling
$2.75 million, $1 million of which he received on
signing the contract.

GOLDEN OUTFIELD Tris Speaker, Harry Hooper, and
Duffy Lewis formed the outfield for the Boston Red
Sox in the years 1910–15. Speaker and Hooper are
both in baseball's Hall of Fame. Lewis played Fenway
Park's left field so well that the incline in front of the
wall was known as "Duffy's Cliff." The trio, which
earned its nickname because of its value to the Red Sox
and its exceptional skills, really glittered in the 1915
World Series. Lewis batted .444, Hooper .350,
Speaker .294, and collectively they accounted for 20
of Boston's 42 hits. The storied outfield was broken up
after the 1915 season, when Tris Speaker was traded to
the Cleveland Indians.

GOLF The "modern" birthplace of the sport of golf is the
fabled St. Andrews course in Scotland, which was established in 1552. The Honourable Company of the
Royal and Ancient Club—the Society of St. Andrews
Golfers—in 1754 formulated the "13 articles" that
form the bedrock of rules of the sport to this day. The
actual word *golf* is allegedly derived from the Scottish
word *goulf* which meant to "strike" or "cuff." As a

noun, *goulf* referred to a "blow." Many generations before the Scots, a form of golf existed. The Roman sport of *paganica* or the Country Game involved players swinging away with a club at a leather-covered ball that was stuffed with feathers. Frenchmen and Belgians knocked away at a wooden ball in their games of *crosse, chole* and *jeu de mail*. The clubs they used came in all sizes, shapes, and textures. Sometimes in the game of *chole*, a leather ball stuffed with hay served as the replacement for the traditional wooden sphere. In other sections of the world, other national groups had games that were primitive versions of golf.

GOLFING IRONS/WOODS   Once upon a time the names of golfing irons and woods were more picturesque, but also more confusing. Why the names changed was mainly for convenience, but for the record here are the approximate match-ups:

Modern Name	Old Name
No. 1 iron	Driving Iron
No. 2 iron	Midiron
No. 3 iron	Driving Mashie
No. 4 iron	Mashie-Iron
No. 5 iron	Mashie
No. 6 iron	Spade Mashie
No. 7 iron	Mashie Niblick
No. 8 iron	Lofter
No. 9 iron	Niblick
No. 10 iron	Wedge
No. 1 wood	Driver
No. 2 wood	Brassie
No. 3 wood	Spoon
No. 4 wood	Cleek

"GOOD FIELD, NO HIT" Mike Gonzalez played major
league baseball for 17 years with a variety of teams.
Born in Havana, Cuba, he had a lot of baseball knowledge but a not-too-effective command of English. It
was during his time as a scout that a phrase that has
become part of the popular language was first uttered
by Gonzalez. He was asked to check on a minor league
ball player and—as the story goes—to telegraph back
his findings to the major league club that had shown
interest. Gonzalez watched the young ball player for a
few days and noted that he could swing the bat but had
defensive shortcomings. And then Gonzalez, saving
time, money, type, and English, sent his scouting re-
port: "Good Field, No Hit."

GORGEOUS GEORGE His real name was Raymond
Wagner and his bleached-blond hair and outrageous
manner in the wrestling ring during the 1950's bedaz-
zled television viewers. Wagner's show-biz personality
and his carefully coiffured tresses helped him earn
more than $250,000 per annum during his better years.
It is believed that Wagner borrowed the nickname of
Georges Carpentier, the elegant French boxer, for
Wagner was anything but "gorgeous" in the ring (see
MILLION–DOLLAR GATE).

GRAND PRIX (RACES) This term is French for "grand
prize." It was first employed in 1863, as a designation
for the one-mile seven-furlong race for three-year-
olds. Today's Grand Prix races denote the 13 races for
single-seater Formula 1 cars. Staged annually in 13
different nations, the points earned figure in for the
world championship for drivers.

GRAND SLAM It is believed that baseball was the first sport to use this term, which is derived from contract bridge (the taking of all 13 tricks). As used in baseball, the term denotes a home run that is hit with the bases loaded. In 1930 the term was used in golf to describe the four major-tournament victories of Bobby Jones— the winning of the British and United States open and amateur championships. His unique accomplishment was also called the Impregnable Quadrilateral. The modern use of the term, which came into vogue after World War II, refers to the winning of the United States Open, the British Open, the Masters, and the United States Professional Golfers' Association Championship by one player in the same year. No golfer has ever won the modern Grand Slam.

   In tennis the term describes the winning of the singles events of the French Open, Australian Open, Wimbledon, and the United States Open by one player in the same year. Its origin is traceable to golf's Grand Slam.

GRAY EAGLE Hall of Famer Tris Speaker played 22 years in the majors and had a lifetime batting average of .344. His nickname came about because of the unique manner in which he played center field. Tris would play very shallow and race back to swoop down on fly balls hit over his head like some mighty eagle going after its prey.

GREAT WHITE HOPE On December 26, 1908, Jack Johnson defeated Tommy Burns to become the first black heavyweight champion. A frenzied search began for the white boxer—the white hope—who could defeat Johnson. An arrogant, sophisticated type, Johnson's exploits with the law and with white women prodded the "white hope" advocates. They even talked Jim Jeffries out of a six-year retirement and got him to fight Johnson. It took the efforts of gigantic Jess Willard through 26 rounds in the heat of Havana on April 15, 1915, to knock out Johnson and claim the heavyweight championship of the world and the title of the Great White Hope.

GREENBERG GARDENS Hank Greenberg closed out his illustrious major league career in 1947 as a member of the Pittsburgh Pirates. A power-hitting right-handed batter, he blasted 25 homers that year—most of them into a section of the outfield that was dubbed Greenberg Gardens.

GREY CUP Albert Henry George Grey, former Governor General of Canada, donated the cup in 1909. It is the championship trophy and the name of the championship game of the Canadian Football League.

GUMP WORSLEY Goalie Lorne Worsley, also known as the Gumper, was a National Hockey League star for the New York Rangers and other teams. A tough, gritty performer, Worsley was given his nickname by a childhood friend who claimed that Worsley resembled the comic strip character Andy Gump.

GYMNASTICS In conquering Greece the legions of Rome discovered the gymnasiums—places where the Greeks exercised (*gymna-zein,* "to exercise naked). The Romans modified the Greek exercises into supplements to their military training and thus indirectly advanced the sport of gymnastics.

H

HACK WILSON A short, red-faced, gorilla-shaped man, Hack Wilson played for the Chicago Cubs from 1926 to 1931. In those years he was an American folk hero—the million-dollar slugger from the five and ten-cent store. In those years he drove in more runs than any other player except for Babe Ruth and Lou Gehrig. He set National League records that still stand for the most home runs and most total bases in a season and the major league record for runs batted in. The stock market crashed in 1929, but the Li'l Round Man soared in 1930: he smashed 56 homers, drove in 190 runs, and batted .356.

The Cubs purchased Robert Lewis Wilson in 1926 from Toledo for $5,000. Dubbed Hackenschmidt, after a famous wrestler of the time, he ripped by day and nipped by night. The Hacker was called the poor man's Babe Ruth because of the $40,000 he earned in 1931—a salary second only to the Babe's. Wilson's batting trademarks were parallel knuckles on a no-nub bat handle, and a booming voice that declared when rival players taunted him, "Let 'em yowl. I used to be a boilermaker and noise doesn't bother me." In 1932 Hack became a Brooklyn Dodger and finished out his career as a member of the so-called Daffiness Boys. It was a perfect climate for the man with so many nicknames, and with the Dodgers he was called the Hacker.

With all his accomplishments, with all the verve he exhibited, with all the fame he had—Hack Wilson was not admitted to the Hall of Fame until 1979.

HAIG, THE Walter C. Hagen was a flamboyant figure and one of the top golfers in the Golden Age of sports—the winner of 11 national championships. His nickname was an affectionate shortening of his last name.

HAMBLETONIAN The main United States trotting race for three-year-olds, this event originated in 1930 and derives its name from the horse that is known as the Father of the Breed. Hambletonian was born on May 5, 1849, foaled by a crippled mare under a bunch of oak trees on a New York farm. In the years 1851–74, Hambletonian sired 1,331 foals. His stud fee began at $25 and then escalated to $500—a record for that time. Ironically, it is reported that 90 percent of the best pacers and trotters have been able to trace their roots back to Hambletonian, who rarely raced and seldom even appeared in harness.

HAMMERIN' HANK Four times he led the American League in home run hitting. In 1938 he blasted 58—and no man had hit more in a season up to that point in time except Babe Ruth. His name was Henry Benjamin Greenberg, but he was better known as Hank Greenberg. He played a dozen years for the Detroit Tigers and finished his career in 1947 with the Pittsburgh Pirates. Greenberg was admitted to baseball's Hall of Fame in 1956 (see GREENBERG GARDENS).

HAMPDEN ROAR The name comes from the location—Hampden Park, the international soccer field at Glasgow, Scotland. An otherworldly noise springs forth from the mouths of the soccer zealots who attend games there. The sound envelops the huge stadium and does strange things to visiting teams. The roar is especially in evidence on the day of the Scottish Cup Final.

HANDBALL Known as the game of fives, since the use of all five fingers was necessary, this sport originated in 10th-century Ireland. By the 1800's, it was one of the national sports of Ireland and was known as "handball," since it involved the use of the hand. Phil Casey is credited with bringing the sport to popularity in the United States. An Irish immigrant who settled in Brooklyn about 1882, Casey was amazed that there were no handball courts and no knowledge of his beloved game. His first handball games were with any willing partners and any willing unused brick walls. Later on, he became the handball king of Brooklyn, raising money, building courts, and training the handballers of the future.

HARMSWORTH TROPHY This trophy was first given in 1903 by Sir Alfred Harmsworth. The event it commemorated was the first international powerboat race, which was run over a distance of 135 miles. Staged generally at Picton, Ontario, or Detroit, the race is usually held at intervals of several years.

HART MEMORIAL TROPHY The National Hockey League trophy awarded to a player who is judged most valuable to his team, this honor originated in 1960, when the original Hart Trophy was retired to hockey's Hall of Fame. The trophy gets its name from Cecil Hart, former Montreal manager-coach.

"HE CAN RUN BUT HE CAN'T HIDE" Joe Louis and Billy Conn fought twice for the heavyweight championship of the world. Conn, the former light-heavyweight champion, had resigned his title to be able to box in the heavyweight division. He met Louis in 1941. Conn, a sleek 174 pounds, was a sharp contrast to the burly Louis, who weighed 199½. At the end of the 12th round, Conn was leading Louis on points. An overconfident Conn then tried for a knockout in the 13th round, but he was knocked out instead as Louis unloaded a rapid combination of punishing blows. World War II intervened and both men served in the army. Their second bout was scheduled for Yankee Stadium on June 19, 1946. Conn bragged that he would easily win the fight, that his speed would be too much for Louis, whom he claimed would not be able to catch up to him. "He can run but he can't hide," was the quiet and confident reply of the Brown Bomber. A crowd of 45,000 paid $1,925,564—making for the second-largest payday in the history of boxing to that point in time. For seven rounds Conn ran. He circled, he danced, he countered, he stayed away from Louis. The crowd booed so much that at times the two boxers had difficulty hearing the bell ring at the end of a round. In the eighth round, coming out of a clinch, Louis landed a left hook to Conn's jaw. He followed up quickly with a barrage of lefts and rights. Conn stumbled, staggered, fell. He was unable to run or to hide—he couldn't get up, and Louis prevailed.

HEISMAN TROPHY An annual award given since 1935 to the best undergraduate collegiate football player in the United States, the trophy gets its name from John W. Heisman. A coach from 1892 to 1928, Heisman was both an innovative figure and a fearsome competitor. Never content with just a winning effort, he once allowed one of his teams to trounce an opponent by scoring 220 points, and this earned him the nickname Shut the Gates of Mercy. Heisman invented the spinner play and the direct snap from center to back. He was instrumental in the movement to legalize the forward pass. Since the day in 1935 when Chicago's Jay Berwanger became the first Heisman Memorial Trophy winner, the award has become one of the most prestigious in all of sports. Its significance was underscored by Mike Garrett of the University of Southern California, who won the award in 1965. "I wanted to be immortal. I figured I could do that by winning the Heisman."

HELMS WORLD TROPHY Sponsored by the Helms Athletic Foundation of Los Angeles, this award originated in 1949. An annual presentation is made to the top amateur athlete from each of the continents. The names of the winners are inscribed on a gold, silver, and bronze trophy that is six feet tall.

HERMANN TROPHY Named for its donor, Robert R. Hermann, chairman of the board of the California Surf of the North American Soccer League and an original member of the league, this award has been given annually since 1967 to soccer's top collegiate player of the year. It is awarded on the basis of votes cast by over 250 college coaches in a poll conducted by the *Sporting News*.

HESITATION PITCH A specialty of Leroy "Satchel" Paige, this pitch came out of a slow windup that had a hitch in it. The ball would came at the hitter at various speeds, causing problems in the timing of a swing and helping Satchel to win many games.

HICKOK BELT Ken Stabler of the Oakland Raiders of the National Football League has won it, and so have Phil Rizzuto, Willie Mays, Arnold Palmer, Lee Trevino, Muhammad Ali, and other legendary professional athletes. Its official name is the S. Rae Hickok Professional Athlete of the Year Award, and the first year of presentation of this belt valued at $15,000 was 1950. The concept of honoring the top pro athlete of the year was dreamed up by Alan and Ray Hickok to perpetually memorialize their father through an annual presentation of the belt named for him and the Hickok Belt Company.

"HIT 'EM WHERE THEY AIN'T" William Henry Keeler played 19 years in the major leagues and finished his career with a .345 lifetime batting average. In 1897 Keeler batted an incredible .432. A reporter asked the diminutive batter, "Mr. Keeler, how can a man your size hit four-thirty-two?" The reply to that question has become a rallying cry for all kinds of baseball players in all types of leagues. "Simple," Keeler smiled, "I keep my eyes clear and I hit 'em where they ain't."

HITLESS WONDERS The 1906 Chicago White Sox had a team batting average of .230, the most anemic of all the clubs in baseball that year. The team's pitching, however, more than made up for its lack of hitting. The White Sox staff recorded shutouts in 32 of the team's 93 victories. The "Hitless Wonders" copped the American League pennant and faced the Chicago Cubs in the World Series. The Cubs of 1906 are regarded as one of the greatest baseball teams of all time; they won 116 games that year, setting the all-time major league mark for victories in a season and for winning percentage. The White Sox continued their winning ways in the World Series, however, trimming their crosstown rivals in six games.

"HIYA KID!" Babe Ruth had a great deal of difficulty in remembering names, and "Hiya Kid!" was his traditional greeting to make up for this shortcoming. However, he once was introduced to President Calvin Coolidge and improved on his traditional greeting by shouting, "Hiya Prez!"

"HOLY COW" New York Yankee broadcaster Phil Rizzuto is an exuberant and excitable individual. Some accuse him of rooting for the home team, but most everyone admits that the Scooter watches and describes baseball through the eyes of a fan. The phrase associated with Rizzuto underscores his amazement at the happenings on a baseball field and is generally his "last word" (see SCOOTER, THE).

HOLLYWOOD HENDERSON Dallas Cowboy strong-side linebacker Thomas Henderson's nickname comes from his flamboyant manner on the playing field and his outspoken comments off the field. He is a showman. When he scores, he dunks the ball over the crossbar—a technique that irritates the opposition and that he claims to have originated. During the 1978 National Football League season, he created headlines by stating that the Los Angeles Rams did not have "enough class" to make the Super Bowl. Hollywood defends his actions: "I just have fun. I mean nothing personal about what I say. I don't like to be dull, or just an old, ugly linebacker."

HOME RUN BAKER If there ever was a baseball player who became a legend because of a nickname, it had to be John Franklin Baker. Admitted to the Hall of Fame in 1955, he had a powerful image but not much in the way of home runs. Baker played 13 years and collected a grand total of 93 homers. His best home-run year was 1913, when he popped 12 round-trippers. Baker's lifetime home-run percentage was 1.6, as compared to Babe Ruth's 8.5, Hank Aaron's 6.3, and Rocky Colavito's 5.8. Powerful press agentry or key home runs in crucial situations have to be the explanations for Baker's nickname. His home-run hitting did not make him deserving of it.

HONDO HURRICANE, THE He was 6'5" and weighed 210 pounds. He came up from the minor leagues to the New York Giants in 1947 with a "can't miss" label.

Clint Hartung batted .309 that first year and this meshed with his Hondo, Texas, birthplace to earn him his nickname. Unfortunately, the hurricane blew itself out. Hartung batted only .179 in 1948 and .190 in 1949. His major league career lasted but six years, and Hartung left with a .238 career batting average and thoughts of what might have been.

HORSE, THE Harry Gallatin starred for the National Basketball Association New York Knickerbockers during the 1950's. Though just 6'6", his bulk and power enabled him to outrebound much taller opponents. In the 1953–54 season Gallatin pulled down 1,098 rebounds, an average of 15.3 per game, to set a record. His strength and stamina earned him his nickname.

HORSESHOE PITCHING The sport of horseshoe pitching had an odd beginning. It can be traced back to the time of the Greeks and the Romans, whose armies at the start of the Christian era found that by shoeing their horses they could get more mileage out of them. When the soldiers unshoed their horses, they pitched away the horseshoes. The spare horseshoes became material to play with for the soldiers and their followers. At first horseshoe competition was a contest to see which participant could throw the shoe the farthest distance—a sort of combined horseshoe and discus-throw event. Then the participants refined the game by throwing the horseshoes at a stake or a post. Out of this came the game of horseshoes.

HOUSE THAT RUTH BUILT This is another term for Yankee Stadium, the ball park in the Bronx that Babe Ruth's home runs made famous. In his prime he acted

as a sort of Pied Piper, wooing fans and tourists alike
to the Stadium to witness his power hitting and power
personality.

"HOW ABOUT THAT" Former New York Yankee broadcaster Mel Allen must have uttered that phrase
thousands of times in noting the spectacular fielding
plays, long home runs, and superb pitching performances that he viewed during his long career. It was a
phrase expressed in an excited Southern accent that
almost made those who heard it want to respond to
Allen and given their opinion of what he had de-
scribed.

I

ICE HOCKEY The first recorded use of the term *ice hockey* appeared in a newspaper account of a contest held at Montreal's Victoria Skating Rink in 1875. But years and years before that, in the little villages and hamlets of Canada, youngsters played on frozen lakes and ponds with sticks made from the branches of trees and pucks formed from frozen "horse apples." Eventually the sport became an indoor game, but its origins can be traced to youth passing wintertime away outdoors.

"IF IT'S UNDER *W* FOR 'WON,' NOBODY ASKS YOU HOW" As a player and a manager, Leo Durocher could invent more ways to tease and taunt and beat the opposition than virtually any other figure in the history of baseball. His was an aggressive, no-holds-barred approach to the National Pastime. The quote attributed to him reflects his attitude toward the game (see LIP, THE).

"I LOST IT IN THE SUN" Billy Loes was a Brooklyn

Dodger pitcher in the 1950's. Possessed with a great deal of natural athletic ability, Loes never achieved the success experts predicted should have come to him as a matter of course. At times he was quicker with a quip than with his glove. During the 1952 World Series, Loes ingloriously misplayed a ground ball hit back to the pitcher's mound. Later he was questioned by a reporter who wished to learn what had been the problem. Loes responded, "I lost it in the sun."

INDIANAPOLIS 500 Staged annually since 1911, this event run in May at the Indianapolis Motor Speedway and sponsored by the United States Auto Club gets its name from its location and the number of miles autos must complete to win the race.

"I NEVER MISSED ONE IN MY HEART" Long-time major league umpire Bill Klem's phrase was his attempt to explain how difficult the job of umpiring was and how objective he always attempted to be. Klem retired in 1941—according to him, after the first time he pondered whether he had correctly called a play.

"IN THE CATBIRD SEAT" Red Barber beguiled Brooklyn Dodger fans for years with his Southern voice, narrative skills, honest manner, and down-home expressions. His pet phrase to describe when someone was pitching, hitting, fielding or just functioning well was a reference to that individual as being in the "catbird seat." Barber also used the phrase to characterize a team ahead by a comfortable margin and virtually assured of victory.

IRON HORSE Lou Gehrig, a.k.a. Larrupin' Lou and Pride of the Yankees, earned his main nickname for playing in 2,130 consecutive games—a major league baseball

record that will probably never be broken. Day in and
day out for 14 years, like a thing made of iron, Gehrig
was a fixture in the New York Yankee lineup. He led
the league in RBI's, 5 times and 13 years he drove in
more than 100 runs a season. The man they also called
Columbia Lou—a reference to his Columbia University student days—was admitted to the Hall of Fame in
1939.

IRON MAN Joe McGinnity pitched in the majors from
1899 to 1908. He started 381 games and completed
351 of them. He had a lifetime earned-run average of
2.64. McGinnity could pitch day in and day out like a
man made of iron. In 1903 he pitched and won three
doubleheaders. Winner of 247 games—an average of
almost 25 a year—McGinnity was admitted to baseball's Hall of Fame in 1946.

"IS BROOKLYN STILL IN THE LEAGUE?" At the beginning of the 1934 baseball season, New York Giant
manager Bill Terry teasingly asked reporters that question about his team's subway rivals. It was a natural if
uncomplimentary query. The Dodgers were still in the
league, but they had not done much in the past few
years. The final two games of the 1934 season saw the
Dodgers still in the league but long out of the pennant
race. On the other hand, the Giants were tied for first
place with the St. Louis Cardinals. Brooklyn's last two
games were with the Giants. Brooklyn won those last
two games, while St. Louis swept its final two games
from Cincinnati to take the National League pennant.
And Giant manager Bill Terry learned the virtues of
letting sleeping dogs sleep. Van Lingle Mungo, the
Dodgers' star pitcher of that year, remembers the way

it was: "Because of Terry's taunt, we wanted to win just a little more each time we played them that year. The fans were even more so; they'd boo Terry every time he'd stick his head out of the dugout." Mungo pitched more innings than any other hurler in 1934, but he especially remembers the last game he pitched and won against the Giants. "It was like a World Series to me. I never wanted to win a game as much. I think it was one of the best games I ever pitched and I pitched it for Bill Terry."

"IT'S NOT OVER 'TIL IT'S OVER" This phrase, attributed to Yogi Berra, underscores the former Yankee great's long experience in the wars of baseball. Berra, as player, manager, and coach, has seen the game of baseball from many levels. A victim and victor of late-inning rallies, of curious changes in the destinies of players and teams, his stoical attitude to the National Pastime is the view of a pro, even though it is expressed in perhaps not the most appropriate syntax.

"IT'S NOT WHETHER YOU WIN OR LOSE, BUT HOW YOU PLAY THE GAME" This line from a romantic poem written by sportswriter Grantland Rice has very nearly become a cliché's cliché, and a rationale for losers. Rice philosophized about sports, likening them to the game of life, and preceded this line with musing about "when the Great Scorer" comes to tally up what you've done, how you played the game shall be a major consideration.

IVY LEAGUE This term refers to the collegiate athletic conference consisting of Brown, Columbia, Cornell, Dartmouth, Harvard, Pennsylvania, Princeton, and Yale.

J

JAI-ALAI The Basque language supplied the name of the sport that is so appealing to many Latins. *Jai-alai* in Basque means "merry festival," and that literally is what the sport is for many—especially for those who bet on the contests and win.

JACK JOHNSON During World War I the German 5.9 inch howitzer, its shell, and its shell burst, derived their common name from John Armstrong ("Jack") Johnson, the first black world heavyweight champ. The German weapon was used against the Allies and its sound, its power, and the thick black smoke that it gave off underscored the force of Jack Johnson, the boxer.

JARRY PARK The Montreal Expos today play baseball in the 70,000-seat Olympique Stadium, a futuristic left-over from the Montreal Olympics. The roots of the team reach back, however, to Jarry Park, their first home. Months before the Expos played their first baseball game, in 1969, a site for the team had not been determined. National League President Warren Giles, Commissioner Bowie Kuhn, Montreal Mayor Jean Drapeau, and Montreal Expos President John McHale came to Jarry Park "as the last thing to look at as a possibility," according to McHale. He continued, "There was an amateur baseball game going on. There was great enthusiasm. As we walked into the park, the people recognized Warren Giles, and they stood up. They cried out: *'Le grand patron. Le grand patron!'* Giles said, 'This is the place. This is the place. This is the only place I've seen where we can play baseball in Montreal.' " The Expos expanded the amateur ball park from the 2,000 seats that existed behind home plate to a facility that accommodated 28,000. In the ninth year of their existence, the Expos left Jarry Park and its *toujours un beau coup* ("a hit every time") baseball for something new. The old park remains for the people of Montreal *une affaire du coeur* ("an affair of the heart").

(HAYES) JENKINS SPIRAL The spiral used in men's figure skating, it is named for the American who was the first person to execute it.

JOCKEY Once upon a time all those in England who dealt with horses were called jock or jockey. As time went on, horse traders who were also horse riders became "jockeys."

JUDO Judo is an outgrowth of ji-jitsu, which came into being in Japan thousands of years ago. At first only

Samurai warriors were permitted to study the sport. By the 1850's different ji-jitsu schools existed all over Japan. Each one went its own way and seemed to have its own secrets.

Professor Jigoro Kano, a man frustrated by the different approaches and by what he saw as the violence of some of the schools, founded what we know today as judo. Kano did this in 1882, calling the new sport *judo,* which means "the gentle way." Out went the dangerous moves such as foot and hand strikes, and in came some of the old ji-jitsu methods together with some new techniques. Many trace judo's start in the United States to President Theodore Roosevelt. A believer in a keen mind and a strong body, Roosevelt witnessed a judo contest and was so impressed that he imported his own Japanese judo instructor.

JUNIOR GILLIAM The Los Angeles Dodgers dedicated the 1978 World Series to James Gilliam, who died at the age of 49 just before the Series began, a victim of a cerebral hemorrhage. There have been many athletes over the years who have been called Junior, but Gilliam seemed to have a lock on the name as he had a lock on the emotions of all of those associated with baseball. He was given the name when he performed as the youngest player on the Baltimore Elite Giants, a black baseball team. There were attempts to retire the name when Gilliam played for the Brooklyn Dodgers and the Los Angeles Dodgers and then coached the L.A. team, but the name endured. In the 1978 World Series, all the Dodgers wore on their uniform sleeve a round black patch with Gilliam's number 19 on it. In the eulogy for the man who was proud he was a Dodger, it was said, "He went through all of his life without ever once getting his signals crossed." Gilliam was "Junior," but he was a big man.

JUNK MAN, THE Eddie Lopat was the premier left-handed pitcher for the New York Yankees in the late 1940's and through most of the 1950's. He recalls how he obtained his nickname: "Ben Epstein was a writer for the New York *Daily Mirror* and a friend of mine from my Little Rock minor league baseball days. He told me in 1948 that he wanted to give me a name that would stay with me forever. 'I want to see what you think of it—the junk man?' In those days the writers had more consideration. They checked with players before they called them names. I told him I didn't care what they called me just as long as I could get the batters out and get paid for it." Epstein then wrote an article called "The Junkman Cometh," and as Lopat says, "The rest was history." The nickname derived from Lopat's ability to be a successful pitcher by tantalizing the hitters with an assortment of offspeed pitches. This writer and thousands of other baseball fans who saw Lopat pitch bragged more than once that if given a chance, they could hit the "junk" he threw (see STEADY EDDIE).

K

KARATE Daruma, an Indian monk, introduced the skills of a martial art to the monks of the Shao Lin monastery in China thousands of years ago. It was taught as a way of developing strength and endurance. Daruma studied animals' fighting positions and blended these with other combat techniques, teaching the Shao Lin monks so well that they became the most fearsome fighters in all of China. A system of instruction was developed to keep the sport fairly secret but at the same time allow it to be passed on to those to whom the monks wished to teach it. The system was based on *kata*—setpieces and techniques of the martial art that Daruma originated.

In the 1600's the feudal lords on the island of Okinawa banned the use of all weapons. The martial art that Daruma developed then spread to Okinawa. It was called "Chinese hand," in tribute to the country where it was first developed. Modern karate was introduced to the Japanese public in 1922 by Master Funakoshi Gichin. He gave it the name *karate,* which means "open hand." Today *shotokan* ("Shoto" was Funakoshi's nickname) is the most widely-practiced and -taught approach to karate in the West.

KENESAW MOUNTAIN LANDIS Judge Landis was baseball's first commissioner. He ruled the sport with supreme authority until 1946. The first part of his name came from the place where his father had been wounded during the Civil War.

KENTUCKY DERBY Held annually at Churchill Downs, in Lexington, Kentucky, since 1875, this premier event is a 1¼-mile stakes race for three-year-old thoroughbred horses. The first race in horse racing's Triple Crown, the "derby" part of its name is derived from the English Derby, which derived part of its name from the Earl of Derby (see DERBY).

KING KONG Charlie Keller played major league baseball for 13 years, all but two of those years with the New York Yankees. Keller was a solid ball player with a lifetime batting average of .286. He was a muscular 5'10", 185-pounder, and his nickname came from the main character of the movie of the same name. Keller's given names were Charles Ernest, but there were many pitchers who believed it was King Kong who was hitting against them.

KING OF THE NETS William Tatem Tilden II, a.k.a. Big Bill, was literally royalty on the tennis courts. One of the great stars of the Roaring Twenties, Tilden's unique style of play featured booming serves and long strides across the court that enabled him to stay back near the baseline. Seven times he won the United States Championship. Eleven times he was a Davis Cup team member. Tilden was the first American to triumph at Wimbledon. When he finally retired, he had won over 70 tennis championships and earned his nickname.

KIPLINCOTES DERBY A five-mile horse race that originated in 1519, this event claims to be the oldest horse race in the world. Staged through several English parishes, the race begins at South Dalton near Beverly, Yorkshire, and ends at Kiplincotes Farm—the site the race derives its name from.

KLU Ted Kluszewski played 15 years in the major leagues. He pounded out 279 homers, recorded a lifetime slugging average of nearly .500 and a career batting average of nearly .300. He was a favorite of the Cincinnati fans; at 6'2" and 225 pounds, his bulging biceps were too huge to be contained by ordinary shirt-sleeves. Kluszewski cut off the sleeves and started a new fashion in baseball uniforms—just as fans and sportswriters cut off part of his name to make for a nickname more easily pronounced and printed.

KRAUT LINE During the late 1930's and early 1940's, Bobby Bauer, Milt Schmidt, and Woodrow Wilson ("Woody") Dumart formed a potent line for the Boston Bruins of the National Hockey League. Their collective nickname came from their shared German heritage.

L

LACROSSE Pierre de Charlevoix, a French cleric, gave the sport of lacrosse its name in 1705. The Algonquin Indians were happily playing a game of their favorite sport, *baggataway,* and the Frenchman was an especially interested spectator. The webbed stick used by the Indians was a particular source of interest to de Charlevoix, who saw in the stick a resemblance to a bishop's *crozier* ("cross"). Ultimately, the French adopted the sport the Indians played and changed the name from *baggataway* to lacrosse.

LE GRANDE ORANGE Rusty Staub played for the Montreal Expos in the years 1969–71. "He came here as an unknown, and not only was he our first big star," Expo President John McHale remembers, "but he had a way of relating to the people and a sense of being a

star. His reddish hair, his physical stature, his un-
selfishness made him an easily identifiable figure. He
was a very important factor in those years in the success of the team." Staub's size, red hair, and personality all merged into the nickname the Montreal fans
coined for him.

LE GROS BILL Jean Beliveau weighed 210 pounds and
was six feet, three inches tall. His heft and height made
him stand out in the scaled-down world of the National
Hockey League, and this was just one reason for his
nickname. His bigness is also seen in his Hall of Fame
membership, his leading Montreal to ten Stanley Cup
championships, his 507 goals in 18 seasons, and his
instinctively correct moves all over the rink.

LEOTARDS Jules Leotard was a French aerial acrobatist
during the 19th century. He invented the leotard cos-
tume and urged other men to wear it: "Do you want to
be adored by the ladies? Put on a natural garb that does
not hide your best features." The Frenchman's original
outfit was a tight-fitting, elasticized one-piece gar-
ment. Although it has been refined over the years,
leotard(s) are used throughout the world of sports by
men and women.

LIGHT-HEAVYWEIGHT BOXING DIVISION Around the
turn of the century, Lou Houseman, a Chicago boxing
promoter, was mainly responsible for creating a new
weight division in boxing called light-heavyweight.
Houseman managed boxer Jack Root, who provided
the starting point for the new division. Root was too
heavy to continue competing in the middleweight division and too light to box in the heavyweight division.

Houseman argued that a weight division with a 175-pound limit would be attractive to fans and a solution to the problems of fighters such as Root. On April 22, 1903, Root won a ten-round decision over Kid McCoy and became the first light-heavyweight champion. On the Fourth of July that year, Root fought George Gardner for the light-heavyweight title. Gardner kayoed Root in 12 rounds and became the champion. And thus began the line of light-heavyweight boxers, which has included Bob Fitzsimmons, Tommy Burns, Battling Levinsky, Gene Tunney, Harry Greb, Battling Siki, Maxie Rosenbloom, Billy Conn, Joey Maxim, Archie Moore, Jose Torres, Victor Galendez, and the "Jewish Bomber," Mike Rossman.

LINKS The term *golf links* is generally applied to any area where the sport is played. However, the word is derived from the Old English *hlinc* ("a ridge of land"), and in its strictest application refers to an area of flat or gently sloping land along a seashore. Virtually all the original golf courses were "links," or courses built on ridges of land along the seashore.

LIP, THE When he was an infielder for the St. Louis Cardinals during the 1930's, Leo Durocher was known as Screechy because of his high-pitched voice and bench-jockeying ability. As he moved through his 17-year playing span and 24-year managing career with the Brooklyn Dodgers, New York Giants, Chicago Cubs, and Houston Astros, Durocher attracted the ire of umpires and the hostility of rivals with what they termed his motor-mouth. A tough, combative, at times profane individual, Durocher's nickname was an apt one.

LITTLE BROWN JUG   This one-mile stakes race for three-year-olds was named for a top pacer who excited improvers of the breed in the years 1881–83. The race has been held annually since 1946 and is one of the contests that makes up pacing's Triple Crown.

LITTLE LEAGUE BASEBALL   In 1939 Carl E. Stotz founded the first Little League in Williamsport, Pennsylvania. Within two decades, kids and parents all over the United States and other countries were competitively involved. Williamsport has been the site of the Little League World Series since 1947.

LITTLE MISS POKER FACE   Helen Wills was one of the great figures in American tennis. She won seven American championships, eight Wimbledon titles, and four French titles. Her nickname came from her sphinxlike behavior on the court. She rarely spoke to an opponent, instead peering out of an expressionless face that was generally topped by a green-lined white eyeshade.

LITTLE NAPOLEON   John J. McGraw came from the old Baltimore Orioles to take control of the New York Giants on July 16, 1902. He inherited a last-place team that had had 13 managers since 1891. The man they called Mugsy immediately released half the players on the roster of the Giants. "With my team," he said, "I'm absolute czar." Driving, cajoling, innovating, McGraw moved the Giants from a last-place finish in 1902 to a second-place finish in 1903. He drove the New York team to a pennant in 1904. In his 30 years as manager, the Giants won ten pennants and finished second 11 times. McGraw's small physical stature contrasted sharply with the giant power that his gait, his face, and his name, projected throughout the world of baseball. He was famous for such lines as "The only popularity I know is to win," "Do what I tell you, and I'll take the blame if it goes wrong," and "I do the hiring and the firing around here." He was little in size but had Napoleonic power, and these two traits merged into the nickname of the man who was one of the greatest managers in baseball history.

LITTLE PROFESSOR Joe DiMaggio's younger brother, Dom, played center field for the Boston Red Sox for 11 years and compiled a lifetime .298 batting average. He wore glasses, was a keen student of the game, and was but five feet, nine inches tall and 168 pounds—and these characteristics supplied the reason for his nickname.

LONG COUNT, THE Gene Tunney had wrested the heavyweight championship of the world away from Jack Dempsey on September 23, 1926, in a battle in the rain in Philadelphia before 120,000 fans. A year less a day later, more than 100,000 people paid $2,658,660 to witness the rematch at Soldier's Field, Chicago. For the first six rounds, the battle was almost a repeat of the first encounter. Tunney kept piling up points, scoring repeatedly with his left hand. In the seventh round, Tunney was caught against the ropes by Dempsey. A solid left hook staggered Tunney. As the champion started to go down, Dempsey flailed away at him, landing seven punishing shots. Tunney went down. It was the first time in his career that he had ever been knocked off his feet. Dempsey stood over the fallen champion anxious to finish him. Referee Dave Barry screamed to Dempsey to go to a neutral corner.

Dempsey recalls, "I should have went back to the right corner but I didn't do it . . . the referee grabbed me and pushed me and shoved me back. Then Tunney got up and won from then on out." Dempsey retired from boxing after that fight.

To this day what happened that September 22, 1927, remains one of the most controversial subjects in all of sports. Dempsey supporters claim the "long count" gave Tunney four extra seconds, for the referee delayed the count, under the rules, until the Manassa Mauler went to a neutral corner. Tunney claimed that "at the count of four I came to and was in good shape. I had six seconds to go. Without the long count I would have had two seconds to go. Could I, in that space of time, have got up? I'm quite sure I could have."

LOS ANGELES LAKERS The nickname for Minnesota is Land of 10,000 Lakes. The nickname for the former Minnesota National Basketball Association franchise was the Lakers, derived from the state they represented. When the franchise was moved to Los Angeles, "Lakers" was kept as the nickname.

LOSING PITCHER One year he won eight games and lost 18; another year he won ten games and lost 20; in 1939 he lost 16, and in 1940 he led the National League in losses with 22. These statistics earned Hugh Noyes Mulcahy his nickname. In a nine-year career, Mulcahy won 45 games and lost 89.

LOUISIANA LIGHTNING The 95-mph speed he can put on a fastball and his Louisiana birthplace have earned for Ron Guidry of the New York Yankees his colorful and alliterative nickname.

LOUISVILLE SLUGGER This bat is named for the Kentucky city that was named for a French king, Louis XVI, in 1780. The Hillerich and Bradsby bat factory has been manufacturing Louisville Sluggers since 1884. One white-ash tree is needed to produce 60 bats. More than 6 million bats are manufactured annually. Major league ball players use 2 percent of the annual production, but each of their bats is built according to precise individual specifications. Babe Ruth's Louisville Slugger model weighed 48 ounces, while the one wielded by Wee Willie Keeler weighed just 30 ounces.

LUGE This sport's name comes from the French word *luge,* which means "sled" and refers to the one- and two-man sleds that are used in competition.

M

MACCABIAH GAMES Judas Maccabeus (d. c.161 B.C.) also known as the Hammer, led the Hasmonean clan's revolt against the edicts of Antiochus IV, which required Jews to worship Greek gods. All of his guerrilla followers were tortured and killed. The games named for Judas Maccabeus originated in 1929 in Czechoslovakia. An international Jewish sports festival staged at approximately four-year intervals, the Maccabiah games resemble the Olympic Games.

MAD HUNGARIAN Al Hrabosky, who arrived in the major leagues with the St. Louis Cardinals in 1970, is a self-created image. Originally a clean-cut pitcher, Hrabosky allowed his hair to grow long and cultivated a beard and a moustache. He then developed a procedure on the pitching mound designed to annoy, frustrate, and sometimes anger batters. He would step off the mound, walk in the direction of second base, pound his glove, talk to himself, trot back to the mound, glower in to the catcher, and release his pitch. Pleasing to the crowds, an aid to, in Hrabosky's phrase, "psyching myself up," the image and the routine have fattened the pitcher's paychecks. There are those who declare that Hrabosky may be Hungarian, but he surely isn't mad.

MAD RUSSIAN Bill Vukovich was only the second man in history to triumph in the Indianapolis 500 two straight years, 1953 and 1954. In 1955, leading after 57 laps and on his way to a third straight win, Vukovich tragically was killed in a crash. His national roots and his charging, aggressive style behind the wheel earned him his nickname.

MADISON The roots for the name of this six-day cycling endurance race go back to the original races that were held for six days in New York City's Madison Square Garden. The current competition is a test of stamina. Two-man teams alternate.

MAHATMA, THE Branch Rickey (1881–1965) was one of baseball's most influential personalities. Inventor of the farm system, the force responsible for Jackie Robinson breaking baseball's color line, the master builder of the St. Louis Cardinal and Brooklyn Dodger organizations, he was elected to the Hall of Fame in 1967. Sportswriter Tom Meany coined Rickey's nickname. Meany got the idea from John Gunther's phrase describing Mohandas K. Gandhi as a "combination of God, your own father, and Tammany Hall."

MALIBU SURFBOARD Malibu Beach, about 25 miles west of Los Angeles, is one of California's top surfing areas. The finned fiberglass surfboard that virtually revolutionized surfing by making acrobatic gyrations possible from a standing position derives its name from Malibu Beach.

MAN, THE (STAN THE MAN) Stanley Frank Musial, St. Louis Cardinal baseball immortal, batted .315 as a rookie in 1942, when he was 21 years old. In 1962, at the age of 41, he hit .330—one point under his lifetime batting average. Musial is the all-time Cardinal leader in games played, runs, hits, doubles, triples, homers, and total bases. His twisted, crouched, coiled stance at the plate enabled him to slash the ball with power or stroke it with finesse to any part of the playing field. Musial was an especially successful hitter in the small confines of Ebbets Field. His specialty was slamming frozen-rope doubles off the outfield walls. Dodger fans had difficulty pronouncing his name, sometimes calling him "Musical." Many of the black Dodger fans simply referred to Musial as "the Man" in tribute to the power and style he displayed. Eventually fans all over the league used this nickname—a reference not only to Musial but to the respect due his power and authority.

MANASSA MAULER Jack Dempsey, heavyweight champion of the world from 1919 to 1926, was born in Manassa, Colorado, from which part of his nickname comes. Knocked out only once in his career (by Fireman Jim Flynn in one round in 1917), Dempsey's power was such that he won 49 of his 77 fights by knockouts, earning the well-deserved reputation as a mauler. Incidentally, his real name was William Harrison Dempsey, but he took the name Jack after a former middleweight of that name (see RING NAMES/REAL NAMES).

MANDRAKE THE MAGICIAN During the late 1940's and into the 1950's, Don Mueller of the New York Giants appeared to have a special gift with a bat in his hands. His lifetime batting average was a respectable .296, yet he never led the league in any hitting category. His nickname came from his expert bat-manipulation and his ability to hit the ball where he wanted it to go.

MAN OF A THOUSAND CURVES His nickname was a bit hyperbolic, but the major league batters who swung at his stuff and came up empty might not disagree with it. For Johnny Sain, talented star of the Boston Braves and other teams, curveball pitches were a trademark and the reason for his nickname. He allegedly had such pitching skill that his curves dropped, darted, hesitated, broke wide, broke fast, broke slow, broke twice. There may not have been a thousand curves, but there were enough variations on these curves Sain possessed that the effect on batters was the same (see "SPAHN AND SAIN AND PRAY FOR RAIN").

MARVELOUS MARV Marvin Eugene Throneberry was perhaps born to be a New York Met. His initials spelled out the name and his personality and limited skills underscored the characteristics of the New York expansion team that made its debut on April 11, 1962. Throneberry, who looked like Mickey Mantle batting but did not get the same results, labored through a

seven-year, four-different-team major league career—
the Mets were his last team. He is a gentle, fine-
humored man, and sportswriters hung the nickname on
him in good-natured jest. Throneberry loved it and
went along with their efforts to depict him as a clown.
Once a teammate dropped an easy fly ball. Marvelous
Marv smiled and shouted, "What are you trying to do
anyway, steal my fans?" A native of Collierville, Tennessee, Throneberry can be viewed today from time to
time deadpanning it through a beer commercial on
television—extracting dividends from his days as a
New York Met.

MASHIE There are quite a few interesting theories as to
how the club that today is called a number 5 iron got its
original name. The Scottish kitchen utensil employed
to make mashed potatoes did not resemble the club in
appearance, but one theory states that what the club did
to a golf ball when used by golfers lacking skill had the
same "mashing" effect. Another explanation for how
the term got its name was provided by J. H. Taylor, a
golfer skilled in the use of the club. Taylor claimed
that when the mashie was first used in 1888, it took its
name from the "mashers" of the time—sophisticated,
modern males who had a way with the ladies. The
club, also new and also sophisticated, took its name
from the play on words off "mashers," he explained.
The simplest explanation for how mashie came to be is
that it evolved from the French word *massue* ("club").

MASTER MELVIN Mel Ott was a power-armed right
fielder for 22 years with the New York Giants. He
smashed 511 home runs in a fabled career that saw him

average better than a hit a game while compiling a lifetime batting average of .304. Ott became a Giant at the age of 16—and that's how his nickname came about. Ott's Hollywood-type beginning was recalled by Eddie Logan, Giants equipment manager, who was about the same age as Ott at the time and was sent to pick up the youth: "We had the 9th Avenue El at the time. Mr. McGraw had told him to ride the El to the last stop, which was the Polo Grounds. He took the El the wrong way and wound up at the Battery. I looked for the straw suitcase. I found him. I said, 'C'mon boy, let's go.' He got the biggest thrill riding back on the train." Labeled "McGraw's baby," Ott was in only 35 games in 1926, then 82 in 1927. "He's too young to play big-league ball," McGraw said, "but I am afraid to send him to the minors and have a manager there tinker with his unorthodox batting style. The style is natural with him. He'll get results as soon as he learns about big-league pitching." And he did.

MASTERS TOURNAMENT The leading United States international golf tournament originated in 1934 at the Augusta, Georgia, National Golf Course. Entry into the tournament is restricted to those invited by the Augusta National Golf Club. Generally participants are picked on the basis of winning a major tournament during the previous year. The Augusta National Club was the creation of golfing great Bobby Jones and his colleague Clifford Roberts. The site of the course formerly was a famous horticultural nursery that covered some 365 acres. The location was ideal for a golf course, with its numerous trees and shrubs and its fertile land. Construction work on the course began in 1931, guided by Jones, who hit hundreds of shots to set up the best positions for hazards, tees, and greens. The first Augusta National Invitation meeting was held in 1934 and was restricted to the current and past winners of tournaments. From this policy came the name Masters. Bobby Jones considered the name too high-sounding, but others liked it and it has remained.

BILL MASTERTON MEMORIAL TROPHY The National Hockey League's award for perseverance, sportsmanship, and dedication to hockey, it was presented to the league in 1966 to honor the name of the late Minnesota North Star player who died that year.

MEAL TICKET, THE Through the long Depression years, one of the great constants in the fortunes of the New York Giants was pitcher Carl Hubbell. The Hall of Famer possessed a left-handed screwball that he threw at different speeds and blended with a dazzling change of pace. He could make the ball almost disappear, so sophisticated was his pitching style. Hubbell won 253 games for the Giants in a 16-year career and notched a 2.97 earned-run average. His nickname came from his value to the Giants. He was a selfless performer. "In a close game, he'd go down to the bullpen and start warming up. He wanted to show that he was willing and ready, and he'd defy the manager not to put him in," recalled former Giant owner Horace Stoneham.

MECHANICAL MAN Famed golfer Byron Nelson was given this alliterative title because of his smoothness and machinelike efficiency on the golf course.

MESSENGER STAKES This one-mile race for three-year-old pacers got its name from the great thoroughbred Messenger. Brought to the United States in 1788, Messenger was an ancestor of many outstanding horses, including Man o' War, Whirlaway, and the trotter Hambletonian. The Messenger Stakes is one of the races in pacing's Triple Crown.

MIGHTY MITE Hall of Famer Miller Huggins played 13 years in the major leagues and managed for 17 more with the Cardinals and Yankees. A 5'6", 140-pounder, his small physical stature and his outstanding playing and managing ability merged into the qualities that produced his nickname.

MILLION–DOLLAR BACKFIELD In 1947 the Chicago Cardinals, the oldest team in the National Football League at that time in terms of continuous operation, won their first championship. The Cardinals were paced by a backfield of Paul Christman (Missouri), Pat Harder (Wisconsin), Charlie Trippi (Georgia), and Elmer Angsman (Notre Dame)—a quartet that because of their worth to the franchise was valued at $1 million. Christman had 17 touchdown passes and more than 2,000 yards in the air in 1947.

MILLION–DOLLAR GATE This phrase describes the amount of money that comes in through the turnstiles, or gate, to witness a live match. There have been several of these mammoth moneymakers over the years, but it took the promotional genius of Tex Rickard and the contrasting images of Jack Dempsey and Georges Carpentier to create the first one. On the afternoon of July 2, 1921, in Jersey City, New Jersey, 80,000 people paid $1,789,238 to see the rough and crude

Manassa Mauler clash with the suave and sophisticated French military hero. It was a press agent's dream fight. It was also the first championship bout that was broadcast on the radio. Carpentier was outweighed by Dempsey by 16 pounds and outclassed in fighting skill, but the crowd was for the underdog they called Gorgeous George and the Orchid Man. Though advised to give the fans a show, Dempsey grew impatient in the fourth round, and after landing a few heavy blows on the Frenchman, knocked him out (see GORGEOUS GEORGE, MANASSA MAULER).

MINNIE MINOSO His real name was Saturnino Orestes Arrieta Armas Minoso, but everyone knew him as Minnie, which made it easier for typesetters, reporters, and fans. Born November 29, 1922, in Havana, Cuba, Minoso played 15 years in the majors, from 1949 to 1964 (he also appeared in one game in 1977, while a coach with the Chicago White Sox).

MIRACLE BRAVES The year was 1914, the year World War I began. The Boston Braves marched from last place in July to the National League pennant by winning 61 of their last 77 games. That accomplishment was only a part of what earned the Braves their reputation as a "miracle" team. In the World Series, the Braves were given no chance to defeat a powerful Philadelphia Athletics team that boasted such pitching stars as Chief Bender, Bullet Joe Bush, Eddie Plank, Jack Coombs, and what was referred to as the "$100,000 infield" of Baker, Barry, McInnis, and Collins. Boston manager George Stallings was confident. "We'll stop them. We're coming and they're going."

Behind their powerful pitching trio of George Tyler, Dick Rudolph, and Bill James, the Braves won the first game, shocking the baseball world, then the next three, to demolish a dynasty and become the first team in the history of baseball to win four straight World Series games.

MIRACLE MAN The manager of the "Miracle Braves," George Stallings, piloted four different teams in a 13-year managing career. He won only a single pennant in all those years—with the 1914 "Miracle Braves"—but the accomplishment was good enough to earn him his nickname.

MISS HIGGINS A major obstacle to women golfers in the early days was their skirts. Billowy and bulky, they made it very frustrating for women to view the ball on the ground, especially with any kind of wind blowing. The problem was solved by an American golfer named Miss Higgins, who devised an elastic encirclement that could be slipped down from the waist to put the skirt in its place. This piece of elastic ingenuity was named after its innovator.

MR. AND MRS. There is a bit of male chauvinist influence attached to the name of this pocket billiards competition. Generally played by a man and a woman, the man is mandated to shoot at the balls in rotation, while the woman is given a handicap and is free to fire away at any ball on the table. A ball's value is equal to its number, and the first team to record 61 points is the winner. It is also worth noting that the mechanical bridge used in pool (many times by men) is referred to as the "ladies' aid."

MR. INSIDE and MR. OUTSIDE In the years 1944–46 the Army football team never lost a game. A major reason for its success was the running abilities of Felix "Doc" Blanchard and Glenn Davis. The duo scored 89 touchdowns between them and averaged a collective 8.3 yards per carry for the Black Knights of Army. Blanchard was possessed of bull-like power and made most of his runs into the inside of the line; he was known as Mr. Inside. Davis used his blazing speed running the ball time after time to the outside of the line; he was known as Mr. Outside.

MR. ZERO Frank Brimsek began his pro hockey career in 1938 and ended it in 1949. Through all those years except one he played for the Boston Bruins. The Hall of Famer was a truly outstanding goalkeeper. His abilities in the net earned him the nickname Kid Zero when he was a youth, and Mr. Zero as he got older. It was said of Brimsek, "If all the pucks stopped by 'Frigid Frankie' were stuck together . . . they would make a solid rubber hose three inches in diameter, long enough to reach from Boston to his home town in Eveleth, Minnesota." Brimsek had 40 career shutouts and a 2.73 goals-against average. Twice he recorded shutouts in three consecutive games.

HAROLD MONAHAN TROPHY Like Billy Fiske, Harold "Bubs" Monahan was a World War II enlistee and a war casualty. He was a promising bobsled pilot who was shot down in his plane over Italy. The trophy in his name is awarded annually to the National AAU two-man bobsledding champions (see BILLY FISKE TROPHY).

MONSTER, THE His size (6'6" and 230 pounds) and his pitching efficiency during his seven-year stint for the Boston Red Sox in the 1960's earned Dick Radatz his nickname.

MOTOCROSS The derivation for this word is the slang French word for motorcycle, *moto,* combined with *cross,* as in the word *cross-country.* The sport has its origins in post–World War II Europe, where riders steered their bikes over rutted, bombed-out roads. Holland was the site of the first official motocross race in 1947. The sport has evolved today into races over natural terrain with sharp turns, steep hills, mud-splattered surfaces. Heats generally last 30–45 minutes. The rider with the best overall points is judged the winner.

MOUNTAIN MAN In 1977 Bill Walton, then a member of the Portland Trailblazers, then adorned with a great deal of red hair on the face and head, and then much publicized for his treks into the solitude of the mountains, was given this nickname. It was short-lived. Although in deed and appearance Walton fit the nickname, he didn't think the nickname fit him. He gently requested all those in the media who were using it to cease and desist. His request was phrased as gently as an almost seven-foot-tall, 200-pound-plus giant could phrase it. The media ceased using the nickname.

MURDERERS' ROW The New York Yankees of 1927 racked up 110 victories, won the American League pennant by 19 games, and wrecked the Pittsburgh Pirates in four straight games in the World Series. The

Yankee lineup included Babe Ruth, who slammed 60 home runs in the regular season and two more in the World Series, as well as Most Valuable Player Lou Gehrig, who hit 47 homers, drove in 175 runs, notched 447 total bases, finished second to Ruth with a .765 slugging percentage. The Yankees also had Earl Combs, the league leader in hits, singles, and triples, and Tony Lazerri and Bob Meusel, both of whom finished among the league's top four base-stealers. Five Yankee regulars batted .300 or better; four regulars drove in 100 runs or more. The team's slugging average was an astonishing .489—and it was "murder" for any pitcher that faced the potent, powerful, packed row of Yankee hitters.

N

NAISMITH MEMORIAL BASKETBALL HALL OF FAME

Dr. James Naismith (1861–1939), a physical education instructor at Springfield College in Massachusetts, invented basketball in 1891. Naismith's chairman gave him the task of organizing some type of game to fill the time between fall football and spring baseball for the class the doctor taught. The only restriction was that the game had to be played indoors, for the students balked at outdoor activities. Naismith at first attempted to adapt outdoor games such as soccer, lacrosse, and rugby to indoor play. This did not work too well. The sports were unsuited to a confined area and resulted in broken windows and damaged players. Naismith finally settled on the idea of a non-contact sport in which players were not allowed to run with the ball. He got the janitor at the college to string peach baskets on the balconies at each end of the gym.

Dividing his 18 students into two teams, he gave them a soccer ball to play with, posted his original "13 Rules" on the gym's bulletin board—and thus solved his problem of a winter game for the students at Springfield College. There were suggestions that the game be called Naismith Ball, but the good doctor was too modest for this. He coined the name *basketball* for the game he invented. In February 1968 the Basketball Hall of Fame was officially opened on the campus where the game was introduced and its name honors the man who was the father of basketball.

NATIONAL ASSOCIATION FOR INTERCOLLEGIATE ATHLETICS (NAIA) Focused on the needs of small and medium-sized institutions, the NAIA's roots reach back to 1937 and an organization called the National Association of Intercollegiate Basketball. In 1940 the NAIB expanded its focus to include most college sports and changed its name to the present NAIA.

NATIONAL BASEBALL HALL OF FAME AND MUSEUM Located at Cooperstown, New York, the site where Abner Doubleday allegedly invented the game of baseball, the Hall of Fame, established in 1939, is the oldest institution of its kind in the United States.

NATIONAL COLLEGIATE ATHLETIC ASSOCIATION (NCAA) The approximately 800-member collegiate sports-governing body traces its roots back to 1905, when President Theodore Roosevelt was concerned with the future of collegiate football. Violence in the sport at that time had many observers demanding its abolition. Roosevelt called a White House conference whose purpose was to attempt to make the sport safer and saner. Out of that conference evolved in 1906 an

116

organization known as the Intercollegiate Athletic Association. In 1910 its name was changed to the National Collegiate Athletic Association. Thus not only was Roosevelt instrumental in helping to save football, but his concern helped create the NCAA, which governs all intercollegiate sports.

NEVELE PRIDE *Nevele* is lucky *eleven* spelled backwards, but the great horse that bears the name was more than lucky: he was the fastest trotter in history. Winner of 57 of 67 starts, one of the top money-winners in harness-racing history, Nevele Pride was sold to stud for $3 million.

NEW ENGLAND TEA MEN This North American Soccer League team made its debut in 1978. The Tea Men derive their name from the franchise owners, Thomas J. Lipton Inc., the tea company. "We didn't start the team to make money," said President Derek Carroll. "We'd eventually like to turn over some money, but that's not why we're into soccer. We want all the people who make Lipton a $600 million corporation—both our workers and our public—to have something to root for. It's as simple as that."

"NICE GUYS FINISH LAST" As baseball player and manager, Leo Durocher prided himself on his combativeness. He schemed, argued, and fought with the opposition—and sometimes with his own teammates. His feelings about "nice guys" as revealed in the quote above, now almost a cliché attributed to him, expressed his baseball philosophy and underscored his attitude toward winning (see LIP, THE).

NIGHT TRAIN LANE A standout National Football League cornerback in the years 1952–65, Dick "Night

Train" Lane played with a daring ferocity and verve. He was a "hitter," and his nickname had its roots in the locomotive explosiveness with which he went after the ball and the ballcarrier. The rhythm of the big-band arrangement of "Night Train" by Buddy Morrow fused with the rhythm that Dick Lane harnessed his playing engine to.

NO–NAME DEFENSE The Miami Dolphins of the National Football League breezed through an undefeated and untied 1972 season and a Super Bowl win over Washington to become the first professional team ever to go through a complete season with all wins. The heart of that team was a defense that allowed the fewest points in the NFL. None of the Miami defenders had any sort of fame or reputation but they functioned as a team, and that's how the nickname came to be. Of special interest was the fact that the five interior offensive linemen—Norm Evans, Wayne Moore, Bob Keuchenberg, Larry Little, and Jim Langer—all had been cut by other teams.

JAMES NORRIS MEMORIAL TROPHY The National Hockey League's trophy for the top defenseman, this award was created in 1953 to honor the former president and owner of the Detroit Red Wings.

NUMBER ⅛ On August 19, 1951, Eddie Gaedel, wearing number ⅛, came to bat for the St. Louis Browns against the Detroit Tigers. Gaedel, who was signed by Browns owner Bill Veeck, walked on four straight pitches and was then replaced by a pinch runner. The next day the American League banned Gaedel, despite Veeck's protests. Gaedel was a midget, only three feet, seven inches tall.

O

OAKS The 12th Earl of Derby, whose name is affixed forever to the English Derby and the Kentucky Derby, established this 1½-mile stakes race for thoroughbred fillies in 1779. The race was named for the Earl's estate, which is near the site of the competition—Epsom Downs, Surrey, England. The Oaks is one of the annual classic English horse races.

OLD ACHES AND PAINS Luke Appling performed for two decades with the Chicago White Sox. A .310 lifetime batting average was just one of the reasons he was admitted to the Hall of Fame in 1964. His nickname stemmed from the numerous real and imagined illnesses he picked up playing in 2,422 games, while averaging better than a hit a game. Appling was born April 2, 1907, and in 1950 was still playing major league baseball, aches, pains, and all.

OLD RELIABLE Tommy Henrich played for the New York Yankees from 1937 to 1950. His lifetime batting average was only .282, but the value of Henrich to the Yankees was in his clutch hitting. Time after time he would come up in a key situation and deliver. His nickname had its roots in his ability to function under pressure and to perform reliably with distinction.

OLE PERFESSOR Hall of Famer Charles Dillon Stengel was an original. Born on July 30, 1890, in Kansas City, Missouri, he played in the majors for 14 years and managed for 25 more—with the Brooklyn Dodgers, the Boston Braves, the New York Yankees (10 pennants), and the New York Mets (four tenth-place finishes). He had seen it all, and in one of his more coherent statements, he said, "This here team won't win anything until we spread enough of our players around the league and make the others [teams] horse-shit, too." The statement underscored the ineptitude of the early Mets. Loquacious, dynamic, vital, Casey could lecture on baseball and life for hours and hours, and that was just part of the reason for his nickname. Actually, in 1914 Stengel held the title of professor at the University of Mississippi, for he spent that year's spring-training coaching baseball at that institution. That's how he really came by his nickname.

OLYMPICS The ancient Greeks staged a celebration in honor of Olympian Zeus every four years from 776 B.C. to 393 A.D. There were competitions in athletics, drama, and music. French educator Baron Pierre de Coubertin was mainly responsible for the 1896 revival in Athens of the athletics section of the ancient Greek festival. Except for three wartime interruptions, the Olympics have been staged every four years since 1896 in different cities throughout the world. In 1924 a special Winter Olympics program was inaugurated.

ONE-ARMED PETE GRAY Born Peter J. Wyshner (a.k.a. Pete Gray) on March 6, 1917, Gray was a long-time New York City semipro star who played in 77 games for the St. Louis Browns in 1945. He actually had only one arm and played center field with an unpadded glove. He had an intricate and well developed routine for catching the ball, removing the ball from his glove, and throwing the ball to the infield.

$100,000 INFIELD That was the price tag and the nickname given to Eddie Collins, "Home Run" Baker, Stuffy McInnis, and Hack Barry, the players who composed the infield for Connie Mack's 1914 Philadelphia Athletics.

ORANGE CRUSH The 1977 Denver Broncos NFL team wore orange-colored uniforms, and its fierce and determined defensive tactics were aimed at throttling the opposing team's offense all over the field. The site of the Orange Crush soft-drink manufacturing plant, Denver the city could be identified with soda pop, just as the Broncos could be identified by the way they popped the opposition.

OUTLAND TROPHY The annual award to the best interior lineman in college football is named in honor of John Outland, University of Pennsylvania All-American guard in 1897 and 1898. The trophy originated in 1946 and its winners have included Dick Modzelewski

(1952), Alex Karras (1957), Merlin Olsen (1961), Bobby Bell (1962), Ron Yary (1967), and Randy White (1974).

OVER-THE-HILL GANG In 1971 George Allen was installed as head coach of the National Football League Washington Redskins. He immediately obtained players who by pro football standards were aged, afflicted, and washed up—but they transformed the Redskins into a contending team. Allen's pickups included Billy Kilmer, Roy Jefferson, Boyd Dowler, Clifton McNeil, Vernon Biggs, Ron McDole, Diron Talbert, Jack Pardee, and Speedy Duncan. These rejected players and others reached back to the days of their prime, playing aggressive, opportunistic football. Collectively the team might have been over the hill, but in many instances the Redskins had it all over the opposition (see "THE FUTURE IS NOW").

Go-Go Chicago White Sox—a July 1951 view of Luis Aloma, Minnie Minoso and Chico Carrasquel

The original Sugar Bowl site, photographed on December 14, 1935

*The Babe—hitting home runs or signing autographs—he did
it with style*

*A view of seven-year-old Ebbets Field in 1920—the crowd
is purchasing tickets for the first game of the World Series*

Eddie Shore—the Babe Ruth of hockey in one of his rare moments of relaxation in uniform on January 28, 1934

An aerial view of Wimbledon with a clear view of the closed-in "centre court" site of finals and star matches

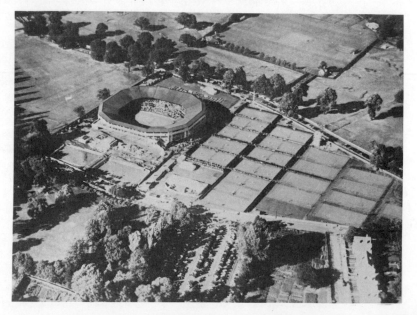

The House That Ruth Built—the old Yankee Stadium

The Wild Horse of the Osage—Pepper Martin demonstrating the art of sliding for St. Louis Cardinal rookies

The Commerce Comet (Mickey Mantle), left, and Old Reliable (Tommy Henrich), right, in Mickey's rookie year of 1951

The Little Napoleon—John J. McGraw in a couple of poses from his playing days

The Davis Cup—the tennis prize that originated in 1900 and is named for Dwight Filley Davis, its donor

The Walker Cup—a prize for which British and American golfers zealously battle

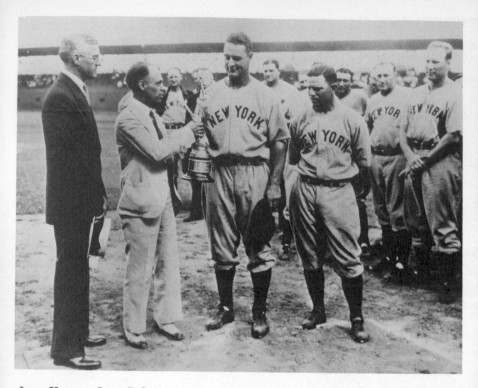

Iron Horse—Lou Gehrig receiving a cup in St. Louis, August 17, 1933, for playing in his 1,308th consecutive major league game—a new record which Lou extended to the all-time 2,130

The Manassa Mauler—Jack Dempsey in training for a defense of his title against Gene Tunney

On the outside looking in—Dizzy Dean and his brother Paul—
suspended by St. Louis Cardinal manager Frankie Frisch in August
1934 for failure to accompany the team to Detroit for an exhibition
game.

*French boxer George Carpentier whose "Gorgeous George"
nickname was appropriated by a wrestler and whose personality
and boxing skills enabled him and Jack Dempsey to draw the
first million-dollar gate in 1921*

The Haig—Walter Hagan, "Grand Old Man of Golf," finishing off a classic iron shot, January 13, 1935

A 50's view of wrestler "Gorgeous George" who is reclining while vacationing in Hawaii

The holder of the world's most famous nick-name and one of the greatest super-stars in the history of sports—PELE

The old and the new—the Jules Rimet trophy permanently retired by Brazil for winning three World Cups. The World Cup presented to the winner of the quadrennial classic.

P

PACIFIC TEN This term describes the collegiate athletic conference that consists of California, Oregon, Oregon State, Southern California, Stanford, UCLA, Washington, Washington State, Arizona, and Arizona State. One of these teams competes each year in the Rose Bowl against a representative of the Big Ten conference. Until the admission of Arizona and Arizona State, effective in 1978, this conference was known as the Pacific Eight.

PACKERS, GREEN BAY The National Football League's Wisconsin franchise was organized in 1919 by Curly Lambeau. The grand sum of $500 was contributed to the new Green Bay team for equipment and uniforms by the Indian Packing Company. And with the money came the team's nickname, the Packers, and permission to use the packing company field for practice sessions.

PADDLEBALL This hybrid racket sport was invented in 1930 by a physical education teacher at the University of Michigan. Earl Riskey peeled off the fuzz from a tennis ball that had been soaked in gasoline to create the first paddleball. He then created a variation of the paddle-tennis racket and the sport of paddleball was on its way.

PADDLE TENNIS The Rev. Frank P. Beal invented this sport in 1898, when he halved the dimensions of a tennis court to create a new game that he thought would be an effective introduction to tennis for children. The sport has changed quite a bit since Beal's time, but it is essentially a scaled-down version of tennis.

PAPA BEAR George Halas, a founder of the National Football League, spent 48 years of his life coaching the Chicago Bears, the team he owned since its founding. His age and his tenure with the team earned him his nickname. In his time he won nine divisional titles and five World Championships. When he retired from coaching in 1968, he said: "I won't miss the detail work, the game analysis, the short list—but the sidelines, the excitement, the decisions—that's what I love." He was a familiar sight at Wrigley Field on Sunday afternoons, jabbering with players and officials, at times virtually transcending the game on the field.

LESTER PATRICK TROPHY The National Hockey League's award for outstanding service to hockey in the United States, it was presented to the league in 1966 by the New York Rangers and named after that team's former coach and manager.

PEARL, THE A slick, smooth ballhandler and imaginative shotmaker, Earl Monroe (also known as Mr. Magic) earned his nickname with his spectacular moves on the basketball court.

PEBBLE PLAY In the 12th inning of the final game of the 1924 World Series between the New York Giants and the Washington Senators, a ground ball that bounced over the head of Giant infielder Freddy Lindstrom led to a score for Washington that gave it the World Championship. It was claimed that the batted ball hit a pebble. "It was never written up the way I looked at it," observed former Giant and Hall of Famer George Kelly. "Now it did hit a pebble, but Fred backed up on it, inexperience. It was his rookie year. This gave the ball an extra hop—the ball played Fred, he didn't play it."

PEEL CUP The oldest soccer trophy in the United States, this cup was donated in 1909 by Peter J. Peel, a leading figure in Illinois soccer, as a fund-raiser for injured players. Today the Peel Cup is awarded to the amateur soccer champion of the state of Illinois.

PEERLESS LEADER, THE Frank Leroy Chance, the first baseman in the famous Tinker-to-Evers-to-Chance Chicago Cub infield trio, was aptly nicknamed. In the years 1906–1911, he led the Cubs to four pennants and two second-place finishes. Functioning as both a player and a manager, Chance recorded 405 career stolen bases—a Cub record—and his clutch hitting and spirited play served as examples of his leadership.

PEE WEE Harold Henry Reese was also known as the Little Colonel, for he hailed from colonel country in Kentucky, but most everyone called him Pee Wee. Various reasons have been advanced for his nickname—he liked playing marbles as a kid; he was small (5'10", 160 pounds); he came up at the same time as Harold "Pistol Pete" Reiser, and writers sought to have the two paired with alliterative nicknames. Whatever the derivation, Reese was anything but small in his influence on the fortunes of the Dodgers, with whom he played for 15 years in Brooklyn and a final year in Los Angeles. He could run, hit, bunt, field, steal, throw, inspire—and most of all win, and influence his team's winning.

PELE (EDSON ARANTES DE NASCIMENTO) Perhaps the most famous of all the nicknames in the history of sports is that of Pele. Strangely enough, even the man who is called by this name does not know how it originated or what it really means. Born October 23, 1940, in Tres Coracoes, Brazil, Pele's life with a soccer ball is the stuff of dreams that began with a stuffed sock. As a poor youth he learned to kick a "soccer ball" that was actually an old stuffed sock. Years later, after scoring his 1,000th goal, he was awarded a four-pound soccer ball made of gold.

Charles de Gaulle made him a Knight of the Order of Merit. A company in Brazil named a coffee after him that in that coffee-mad land became a bestseller. In 1960, after several European countries offered him $1 million to sign with their clubs, the government of

Brazil declared him a national asset, making it impossible for him to leave Brazil without official permission. Pele's power and prestige was such that the Nigerian-Biafran war was halted for a day to allow Pele and his teammates to play a game and then depart without incident for more peaceful surroundings. Pope Paul VI told him, "Don't be nervous my son. I am more nervous than you for I have been waiting to meet Pele personally for a long time." The Pope, like millions of others, knew Edson Arantes de Nascimento by his nickname.

The only player to have performed on three World Championship soccer teams—in 1958 (as a 16-year-old), 1962, and 1970—Pele averaged a goal a game in international competition and broke virtually every record in Brazil's soccer books. Ninety-three times he scored three goals in a game; 31 times he scored four goals in a contest; six times he recorded five goals in a match; and once he knocked in eight goals in a game. He scored more goals than any other player in the history of soccer. So valuable were his legs that they were insured for £20,000.

His signing of a three-year contract with the New York Cosmos on June 10, 1975, just 250 days after retiring from his Santos, Brazil team, resulted in part from the efforts of former Secretary of State Henry Kissinger. The Secretary had told the Brazilian government that Pele's signing to play soccer in the United States would do much to improve international relations.

Soccer's legend retired on October 1, 1977, after his

mission of giving the sport momentum in the United States was concluded. He was called O Rei in Brazil, La Tulipe Noire in France, El Peligor in Chile, Il Re in Italy, O Vasilas in Greece, and King Pele wherever soccer zealots gathered. The power, passion, and personality of the man made most everyone forget his real name, Edson Arantes de Nascimento, and virtually everyone aware of his nickname, PELE.

PENGUIN, THE A Tacoma, Washington, native, Ron Cey of the Los Angeles Dodgers is one of major league baseball's top third basemen. His awkward movements when walking and, especially, when running have resulted in his nickname.

PHANTOM FINN Paavo Nurmi was one of the greatest of all long-distance runners in the history of sports. Allegedly the first man to run with a stopwatch in his hand, the athlete called the Flying Finn set 22 world records in 1920–31. His most outstanding achievements came in the 1920, 1924, and 1928 Olympics. A native of Finland, Nurmi's nickname derived from his ability to disappear from the rest of the field while excelling in long-distance competitions.

PING-PONG The sport of table tennis was invented in 1899 by engineer James Gibb. A founding father of the American Amateur Athletic Union, Gibb fashioned a crude beginning for the sport by fastening a piece of string at the midpoints of the sides of a table. He then obtained a rubber ball and, using members of his family as partners, played the first table-tennis games by hitting the rubber ball back and forth over the string. The sport has gone through several refinements since that time, but James Gibb's basic idea still forms the foundation for the game. The phrase "Ping-Pong" has negative overtones for table-tennis zealots, even though the general public recognizes the phrase as one that realistically describes the sound made when the ball is hit.

PIRATES, PITTSBURGH Pittsburgh entered the National League in 1887, assuming the Kansas City, Missouri, franchise. Regaled in garish, striped baseball uniforms at the start, the team was called the Potato Bugs, Zulus, Smoked Italians, and Alleghenies. In 1891 the team acquired a player many people thought they shouldn't have when they signed one Louis Bierbauer off the roster of the defunct Philadelphia A's of the American Association. Bierbauer became a *cause célèbre* in the National League baseball of that other century. Pittsburgh was castigated for allegedly "pirating" Bierbauer. Not much happened after that as far as Bierbauer was concerned—he hit .206 that year—but he was the "loot" that earned the Pittsburgh franchise the name Pirates.

PISTOL PETE MARAVICH From 1967 to 1970 Louisiana State University's Pete Maravich, a skinny guard with floppy socks, was the leading collegiate basketball point-scorer in the United States. He scored nearly 4,000 points, averaging almost 45 points a game, during his varsity career. Press Maravich, his father and also his LSU coach, gave him his nickname. It was a reference to the young Maravich's quick-trigger shot release and his scoring ability. Pistol Pete continued his illustrious career with the Atlanta Hawks and then the New Orleans Jazz of the NBA. Scoring, passing the ball between his legs or behind his back, showing off a bewildering variety of shots, Maravich became one of the top guns in pro basketball. He was immortalized in "The Ballad of Peter Maravich," written by Woody Jenkins:

> Maravich, oh Maravich,
> Love to fake, love to score,
> Love to hear the people roar.
> Just a boy of 22,
> You made a name at LSU.

PISTOL PETE REISER He played only a decade of major league baseball, less than 1,000 games, but Harold Reiser exploded like a pistol on the fans and players of baseball in the early 1940's. In his second season (1941), he led the National League in batting (.343), and twice he was the stolen-base leader. Tragic collisions against the outfield walls in St. Louis and then in Brooklyn damaged him, slowed his talent, and reduced his skills. There are those who still wonder how great he might have been if not for the pounding he took against those unpadded outfield walls.

PEOPLE'S CHERCE, THE Fred "Dixie" Walker compiled a .306 batting average in an 18-year major league baseball career, with five different teams. From 1940 to 1947 he starred in the outfield for the Brooklyn Dodgers and won the affection of the fans at Ebbets Field. The team had bigger stars, more proficient players, but Walker somehow had a rapport with the fans that made him their favorite and earned for him his "Brooklynese" nickname.

POCKET ROCKET, THE Henri Richard was Maurice
Richard's younger brother. Maurice was born on
August 4, 1921, and Henri on February 29, 1936.
Henri, younger and smaller than his famous brother,
who was called Rocket Richard, was a "pocket" or
lesser version of Maurice—but then there were very
few National Hockey League players who weren't (see
ROCKET, THE).

PODOLOFF CUP A trophy awarded annually to the National Basketball Association's Most Valuable Player,
it is named in honor of Maurice Podoloff, the first
commissioner of the NBA, who was, curiously, just
five feet tall.

POES OF PRINCETON In 1899 the Princeton football
team had a half-dozen players who answered to the
name of Poe. All of them were great-nephews of poet
Edgar Allan Poe.

POLO The sport and its name allegedly date back to 1862
and an exhibition of riding that was staged for British
army officers by Indian horsemen. One of the tricks
displayed by the riders was the ability to hit a ball with
a stick while moving the mount at top speed. The ball
was a bit odd-looking, and the Englishmen learned it
was made from *pulu,* or willow root. Some days later
the British officers decided to emulate the riding tricks
of the Indian horsemen, and especially the techniques
of hitting the ball. From this stemmed the new game
pulu, which as refined became polo.

POLO GROUNDS During the 1880's, the National League
baseball team was known as the New Yorkers. There
was another team in town, the New York Metropoli-

tans of the fledgling American Association. Both teams played their season-opening games on a field across from Central Park's northeastern corner at 110th Street and Fifth Avenue. The land on which they played was owned by *New York Herald Tribune* publisher James Gordon Bennett. Bennett and his society friends had played polo on that field and that's how the baseball field came to be known as the Polo Grounds. In 1889 the New York National League team moved its games to a new location at 157th Street and Eighth Avenue. The site was dubbed the new Polo Grounds and eventually was simply called the Polo Grounds. Polo was never played there.

POWDER PUFF DERBY In 1947, before the days of women's liberation, the International Air Race for Women was inaugurated. The international organization of women pilots, the Ninety-Nines, was responsible for the creation of the race. It is alleged that some macho males were responsible for the nickname Powder Puff Derby, but the women pilots today use the name with pride.

PREAKNESS, THE One of the races in the thoroughbred Triple Crown, this is a $^{13}/_{16}$-mile stakes race for three-year-olds that originated at Pimlico Race Course in Maryland in 1873. The race was staged there until 1889. After being held at a different track, the Preakness has been run on a regular basis at Pimlico since 1909.

PRINCE OF DRIBBLERS Stanley Matthews retired from first-division English soccer five days after his 50th birthday, in 1965. During his prime, in the 1930's,

Matthews' magic moves enabled him to run with the ball at will around any defender he came near. His passing, peerless footwork, and shifty moves with a ball seemingly attached to his foot by an invisible string, earned him his royal nickname.

PRODUCTION LINE Ted Lindsay, Gordie Howe, and Sid Abel are remembered in Detroit and throughout hockey as the trio that teamed up on the same line to produce many goals and seven league titles in a row in the late 1940s and early 1950's. Their scoring and title-producing play gave them their nickname.

PUDGE HEFFELFINGER Three-time all-American at Yale (1889, 1890, 1891), William Walter Heffelfinger was a "lineman's lineman." Called Pudge by his friends because of his six-foot, 200-pound-plus frame, and One-Man Army by the opposition, the Yale standout had the speed and power to enable him to singlehandedly break up play after play.

PUGILISM Sometimes used as a more erudite word to describe the sport of boxing, this term is derived from the Latin *pugil,* meaning "one who fights with his fists." The shorter version of the word is *pug,* which describes a boxer. *Pug-nosed* also comes from the same root.

PUNCH LINE The Montreal Canadiens of the National Hockey League finished first four straight times in 1944–47 and took the Stanley Cup championship in 1944 and 1946. A big part of the team's success was the scoring power and playing ferocity of the line of Maurice Richard, Elmer Lach, and Toe Blake. The line had clout, and that was the reason for its nickname.

Q

QUEENSBERRY RULES The eighth marquis of Queensberry, John Sholto Douglas (1844–1900), a boxing fan, collaborated with lightweight boxer John Graham Chambers to devise some rules to make the sport they loved a bit more humane. For the England of their time featured bare-knuckled, brutal boxing brawls that caused scores of deaths and many injuries. They produced a set of 12 rules that mandated the use of boxing gloves, the ten-second knockout count, three-minute rounds, and the banning of gouging and wrestling. Codified in 1867, generally in effect in all matches by 1875, and made standard in 1889, the dozen rules became known as the Queensberry Rules. Modern boxing is largely regulated on the basis of the Queensberry Rules. And to this day, the name for the rules drawn up with the help of the Marquis of

Queensberry are words synonymous with fair play and playing by the rules in all sports. The original rules were as follows:

1. To be a fair, stand-up boxing match in a 24-foot ring, or as near that size as practicable.
2. No wrestling or hugging allowed.
3. The rounds to be of three minutes' duration, and one minute's time between rounds.
4. If either man falls through weakness or otherwise, he must get up unassisted, ten seconds to be allowed him to do so, the other man meanwhile to return to his corner; and when the fallen man is on his legs, the round to be resumed, and continued till the three minutes have expired. If one man fails to come to the scratch in the ten seconds allowed, it shall be in the power of the referee to give his award in favor of the other man.
5. A man hanging on the ropes in a helpless state, with his toes off the ground, shall be considered down.
6. No seconds or any other person to be allowed in the ring during the rounds.
7. Should the contest be stopped by an unavoidable interference, the referee to name the time and place as soon as possible for finishing the contest; so that the match must be won and lost, unless the backers of both men agree to draw the stakes.
8. The gloves to be fair-sized boxing gloves of the best quality, and new.

9. Should a glove burst, or come off, it must be replaced to the referee's satisfaction.
10. A man on one knee is considered down, and if struck is entitled to the stakes.
11. No shoes or boots with springs allowed.
12. The contest in all other respects to be governed by revised rules of the London Prize Ring.

R

RABBIT MARANVILLE Walter James Vincent Maranville's nickname was rooted in his slight size (he was 5'5" and 155 pounds) and the way he scampered around the bases and sprightly played his shortstop position throughout a 23-year major league career. Maranville averaged approximately one home run per year throughout his career, but he more than made up for his power deficiency by averaging nearly a hit a game. He stole 291 bases and scored more than 1,200 runs—part of the reason for his nickname and his Hall of Fame admission in 1954.

RAJAH, THE Baseball Hall of Famer Rogers Hornsby had a lifetime batting average of .358 and was one of the few men in baseball history to bat .400 three times. Hornsby gained his nickname through what some claimed was a contemptuous pronunciation of his first name—a less-than-appealing reference to his petulant personality. One of the greatest hitters of all time, Hornsby would not go to the movies or read newspapers for fear of straining his keen vision and thus marring his ability to select the right pitches to swing at. He was a regal and special talent and personality.

RAPID ROBERT Hall of Famer Bob Feller pitched for the Cleveland Indians for 18 seasons, winning 266 games. In his major league debut, on August 23, 1936, the Van Meter, Iowa, farm boy, then 17 years old, struck out the first eight men to face him and then seven more, for a total of 15—one short of the then–league record. The blazing speed and power he was able to put on his fastball earned him his nickname. The 12 one-hitters and three no-hitters that Feller recorded in his career helped earn him his reputation as one of baseball's premier hurlers.

READING RIFLE, THE Carl Furillo played 15 years for the Dodgers and for most of those years was a virtual fixture in right field. He was born in Stony Creek Mills, Pennsylvania, close to Reading, and this, coupled with the power of his throwing arm, earned him his nickname. He was also known as Skoonj, a corruption of the word *scungilli,* which was a favorite dish of the Italian-American player.

REAL MCCOY, THE Norman Selby was his real name, but he advertised himself as Charles "Kid" McCoy. Welterweight champion from 1896 to 1899, McCoy's lifetime record was 81 wins (35 of them by knockouts), 6 losses, and 18 draws. There are a few versions as to how the term *the Real McCoy* came into being. One version explains that when the Kid was in his boxing prime and sipping away quietly in a barroom, he heard a bragging voice shout, "I can lick any of the McCoys around, anytime, any place." McCoy took the braggart up on his boast, and kayoed him. Awakened some time later, the now-subdued braggart said: "I meant I could beat any of the fighters around using the McCoy name—not the real McCoy himself." Another story runs along the lines of a drunk challenging the Kid in another barroom scene, yelling, "If you're the real McCoy, prove it with your fists." The Kid proved it. The drunk went down for a long count. When he awakened, he allegedly said, "That's the real McCoy, all right." In most of his fights, the advertisements always promised that "the real McCoy will appear," and although he was really Norman Selby, he was indeed the Real McCoy.

RENS, THE Their full name was the Renaissance Big Five, and in the period 1932–36 there was no better basketball team in all the United States. Organized in 1922 in Harlem by Bob Douglas, and disbanded in 1948, the Rens were an all-black, independent team that consisted of Clarence "Fat" Jenkins, Bill Yancey, John "Casey" Holt, James "Pappy" Ricks, Eyre "Bruiser" Saitch, Charles "Tarzan" Cooper, and Wee Willie Smith. They played one-night stands, traveled and slept in their own bus, played all types of teams under all types of circumstances. In 1933–34 they posted a record of 88 straight wins and completed the year with a 127–7 record. In 1932–36 the Rens won 473 games

and lost only 49. Basketball's Hall of Fame elected the
entire team to membership in 1963.

RING NAMES/REAL NAMES Boxing is a form of show-
business. Some would say that it is all show-business
today. Nevertheless, over the years boxers, like
show-business personalities, have changed their real
names to more dramatic, more easily remembered, and
more pronounceable ring names. Some significant
examples follow:

RING	*REAL*
Lou Ambers	Louis D'Ambrosio
Henry Armstrong	Henry Jackson
Tommy Burns	Noah Brusso
Kid Chocolate	Eligio Sardinias
Jack Delaney	Ovila Chapdelaine
Tony DeMarco	Leonard Liotta
Jack Dempsey	William Harrison Dempsey
Jack ("Nonpareil") Dempsey	John Kelly
Joe Dundee	Samuel Lazzaro
Johnny Dundee	Joseph Carrora
Vince Dundee	Vincent Lazzaro
Jackie Fields	Jacob Finkelstein
Tiger Flowers	Theo Flowers
Joe Gans	Joseph Gaines
Kid Gavilan	Geraldo Gonzalez
Joey Giardello	Carmine Tillelli
Rocky Graziano	Rocco Barbelo
Beau Jack	Sidney Walker
Jack Johnson	John Arthur Johnson
Stanley Ketchel	Stanislaus Kiecal
Benny Leonard	Benjamin Leiner
Battling Levinsky	Barney Lebrowitz
Joe Louis	Joe Louis Barrow
Rocky Marciano	Rocco Marchegiano

RING	*REAL*
Joey Maxim	Joseph Beradinelli
Kid McCoy	Norman Selby
Archie Moore	Archibald Wright
Willie Pep	William Papaleo
Ray Robinson	Walker Smith
Jack Root	James Ruthaly
Barney Ross	Barnet Rasofsky
Jack Sharkey	Joseph Paul Zukauskas
Dick Tiger	Dick Ihetu
Gene Tunney	James Joseph Tunney
Jersey Joe Walcott	Arnold Raymond Cream
Chalky Wright	Albert Wright
Tony Zale	Anthony Zaleski

ROAD RUNNER II Even nicknames have been protected by the law. The Atlanta Braves signed an agreement with Warner Brothers that granted the Braves the right to call one of their baseball players "Road Runner II," after the cartoon character. The agreement made it illegal for any other athlete to use the name.

ROCKET, THE Maurice Richard—scorer of 544 lifetime goals, the first to notch 50 goals in one season, National Hockey League Hall of Famer, a tempestuous, talented, brawling player—earned his nickname. Former star goalkeeper Glenn Hall explains part of the reason why: "What I remember most of all about the Rocket was his eyes. When he came flying toward you with the puck on his stick, his eyes were all lit up, flashing and gleaming like a pinball machine. It was terrifying" (see POCKET ROCKET, THE).

RODEO The Spanish word for "cattle market," *rodeo,* was an entertainment feature built into the lives of post–Civil War cowboys. Prescott, Arizona, was the site of the first formalized rodeo.

"ROOTING FOR THE NEW YORK YANKEES IS LIKE ROOTING FOR GENERAL MOTORS" During the 1950's the New York Yankees, powered by Mickey Mantle, Whitey Ford, Phil Rizzuto, Allie Reynolds, Jerry Coleman, Yogi Berra, Eddie Lopat, Elston Howard, Bill Skowron, and others, won eight World Series. They seemed to get better, to acquire more and more talent each year, to win with amazing regularity—even monotony. This line attributed to an anti-Yankee—and perhaps an anti-corporate-giant—fan, underscored the mechanical, profitable winning ways of the New York team.

ROPE-A-DOPE This name and technique, both allegedly invented by Muhammad Ali, denoted a style of boxing in which Ali would alternately fight toe-to-toe with an opponent and then rest against the ropes, taking the opponent's punches. The strategy behind this maneuver was to give Ali a chance to rest and to make the opponent "dopey," or arm-weary, from throwing punches that did little damage to Muhammad.

ROSE BOWL The Tournament of Roses has been celebrated every New Year's Day since 1890 with floats and pageantry in an idea inspired by the Battle of Flowers at Nice—a feature of that city's carnival festival held in the last days before Lent. On January 1, 1916, Pasadena, California, held a football game to tie in with its Rose Festival. The game was staged in the Pasadena Bowl, where Washington State trimmed Brown, 14–0, to give American collegiate football

what has been called the "first of the Bowl Games."
(Actually, the first bowl game took place in 1902;
Michigan trounced Stanford, 49–0.) The event was
known as The Tournament of Roses Association Game
until 1923, when the Rose Bowl stadium was erected
and given its name by Pasadena's Harlan W. Hall.

ART ROSS TROPHY The National Hockey League's
award for the leading point-scorer, it was presented to
the league in 1947 in the name of former Boston
manager-coach Arthur Howie Ross.

ROZELLE RULE National Football League Commissioner
Pete Rozelle is credited with instituting this rule,
which bears his name. It requires a team that signs a
free agent who has played out his option to give the
player's former team mutually agreed-on compensation. If this is not possible, the commissioner of the
league determines the compensation.

RUGBY In 1823 a game of football (known to Americans
as "soccer") was being fiercely played at Rugby College in England. One of the players, William Webb
Ellis, broke a rule of the game by picking up the ball
and running with it, thus creating one of the more
historic moments in sports. The play was nullified and
Ellis was censured. Later, after much debate and discussion about what the youth had done, the school's
officials decided that he had a good idea. Rugby College thus invented a new rule and a new game—rugby
football. Close by the Rugby playing grounds is a tab-
let that celebrates the event:

This stone commemorates the exploit of William
Webb Ellis, who, with a fine disregard for the

rules of football as played in his time, first took
the ball in his arms and ran with it, thus originating the distinctive feature of the Rugby game.

RUN FOR THE ROSES On the first Saturday in May each
year, the greatest of the three-year-old colts compete
against each other in the Kentucky Derby. In addition
to the prize money and the prestige, the winning horse
has a horseshoe-shaped garland of roses placed around
his neck. The "run" is thus not only for the money and
the prestige, but also for the "roses."

RYDER CUP American and British golf pros competed un-
officially against each other in 1926. The British team
won 13 matches, lost one, and tied one. The "American" team included three Britishers and one Australian. And despite the lopsided score, the competition
was well received. Samuel Ryder (1859–1936), a
prosperous seed merchant, agreed to donate a gold cup
to symbolize a competition to be held every two years
between the United States and Great Britain. Valued at
£750 back then, the cup and the competition named for
Samuel Ryder have grown much in value since that
time. The first Ryder Cup matches were held at
Worcester, Massachusetts. The United States won nine
matches, Britain two, and one match was tied. During
his lifetime Ryder, the man, was known not only for
the cup he donated but also for his generous aid for the
expenses of the British teams.

S

ST. LEGER Named for Colonel Barry St. Leger, who originated the race in 1776, this 1¾-mile stakes race for three-year-old thoroughbreds comprises one-third of the English Triple Crown. It is an annual competition staged at Doncaster, Yorkshire, England.

ST. LOUIS CARDINALS Originally, during the Gay Nineties, the St. Louis National League baseball entry was known as the Browns. Then they were known as the Perfectos. That was a misnomer, for in the years 1892–99 they finished 12th three times, 11th three times, tenth once, ninth once, and eighth once. In 1899 their owner, Chris Von Der Ahe, decided that perhaps a new look in uniforms might help. The team was outfitted in flashy new fabric accentuated with red trim and red stockings. From the new look came the new name—The Cardinals.

SALCHOW Swedish skater Urich Salchow was the first to execute this skating jump that bears his name. It is basically a leap from the back inner edge of one foot and a full turn in the air to a landing on the back outer edge of the other foot.

SATCHEL PAIGE On July 9, 1948, Leroy Robert Paige, better known as Satchel Paige, arrived on the major league baseball scene as a rookie pitcher for the Cleveland Indians. He gave his official age as "42???" Satchel won six games that year, lost only one, and compiled a fine 2.48 earned-run average. A long-time star in the Negro Leagues—there are estimates that he pitched 33 years, winning more than 2,000 games—Paige traveled all over the world to play baseball. By car, by bus—some say by horse—wherever there was a game, Satch was there. His nickname came from the fact that for most of those years he lived out of his "satchel," or suitcase. He claimed his secret of success was that even though "I got old my arm stayed 19." Paige wore the name "Satchel" on his uniform and billed himself as "The World's Greatest Pitcher." A bone-thin 6'3" with size 12 flat feet, he was opposed to exercise. "I believe in training," he joked, "by rising gently up and down from the bench."

SAY HEY Both a greeting and a nickname—and also a condition—this term belonged to Willy Mays. Regarded by many as the greatest player baseball has ever known (and in 1979, voted into the Hall of Fame), Mays pounded 660 homers and over 3,000 hits (better than a hit a game), scored over 2,000 runs, drew nearly 1,500 walks, drove in nearly 2,000 runs, and compiled a lifetime batting average of .302. The image of Mays in a Giants uniform stealing a base, hitting the ball out of the park, racing back to make a sensational catch running out from under his cap—all underscore the verve of the man they called the Say Hey Kid.

"SAY IT AIN'T SO, JOE" This often-repeated question, used frequently in song and story, had its origins in the emotions of a little boy. After the 1919 Chicago "Black Sox" World Series scandal, a lad walked up to Shoeless Joe Jackson, one of the accused players. The boy posed the above question to his idol (see BLACK SOX and SHOELESS JOE).

SCOOTER, THE Phil Rizzuto pedaled about at shortstop for 13 years as a member of the New York Yankees. His small stature (5′6″, 150 pounds) and his agile ways in the field earned him his nickname (see "HOLY COW").

SCUBA This term is an acronym for "Self-Contained Underwater Breathing Apparatus," which consists of an open-circuit compressed-air system and a closed-circuit oxygen rebreathing system. In 1943 the Aqua-Lung was first successfully developed and tested by Jacques-Yves Cousteau and Emile Gagnan. This independent breathing device enables a diver to obtain compressed air through a hose attached to a metal tank strapped to his or her back. The demand regulator, a valve, reacts to the breathing of the diver. The exact volume of air that is needed by the lungs is then fed to the diver to withstand increased pressure under water. Common usage incorrectly applies the label SCUBA solely to the Aqua-Lung.

SHEA STADIUM On October 17, 1960, the National

League awarded a New York City baseball franchise to a team that would be known as the Mets. That October day was the culmination of the efforts of a special Mayoral Committee appointed to find a way to return National League baseball to New York. Attorney William Shea headed the committee. The Mets' stadium, located in Flushing Meadows, Queens, near the site of the old World's Fair, is named for the man who was instrumental in acting as the godfather of the New York Mets.

SHOE, THE Willie Shoemaker is acknowledged by most experts to be the most successful jockey in history. He has ridden more winners than any other jockey. A shade under five feet tall, a shade under 100 pounds, the fabled rider weighed only 2½ pounds when he was born. His nickname is a shortening of his last name and a kind of romanticized play on words for what he has been able to do with a horse.

SHOELESS JOE Joseph Jefferson Jackson played 13 years in the major leagues for the Philadelphia A's, Cleveland Indians, and Chicago White Sox. His lifetime batting average was .356, third highest in baseball history. He will forever be remembered as one of the eight White Sox players of 1919 accused of throwing the World Series. On the lighter side, Jackson was an illiterate hillbilly from South Carolina who played most of his baseball before he came to the majors without benefit of spikes or shoes—and that's how his nickname came to be. It has been suggested that he was the model for Joe Hardy of Hannibal, Mo., the main character in the play *Damn Yankees* (see BLACK

SOX and "SAY IT AIN'T SO, JOE").

SHOT HEARD 'ROUND THE WORLD (DAT DAY; MIRA-CLE AT COOGAN'S BLUFF) On October 3, 1951, at 3:58 P.M. in the Polo Grounds in New York City, in the last game of the play-off's last inning, Bobby Thomson pounded a one-strike fastball thrown by Ralph Branca. The ball went out on a low and curving line and landed 315 feet away from home plate in the stands. The Polo Grounds exploded with frantic fans and excited ball players. On the radio, New York Giant announcer Russ Hodges screamed out eight times in a row, "The Giants win the pennant! The Giants win the pennant!" Not only had the Giants come from 13½ games back in mid-August to this moment, they had beaten their arch-rivals, the great Brooklyn Dodgers, by scoring four runs in the bottom of the ninth inning. On the streets of New York City, the word went out. In Brooklyn there was sadness, and comedian Phil Foster referred to the time as "Dat Day" in his best alliterative Brooklynese. Others called it the Shot Heard 'Round the World, while Giant fans were content to savor the moment as the miracle that took place at Coogan's Bluff, the geographical region the Polo Grounds was located in.

SILVER FOX Former coach and manager of the New York Rangers, cofounder of hockey's Pacific Coast League, Lester Patrick came by his nickname because of the whiteness of his hair and his crafty ways. A member of the hockey Hall of Fame, Patrick also was honored by the naming of an entire hockey division after him.

SILVER SCOT Despite the loss of sight in one eye as a result of a World War I gas attack, Tommy Armour stands as one of golf's legends. His silver hair and the fact that he was born in Scotland led to his nickname.

SINGER THROWING MACHINE Bill Singer's time as a pitcher in the major leagues, from 1964 to 1973, saw him compile a record of 89 wins and 90 losses. His nickname was a play on words with the Singer sewing machine.

SLAMMIN' SAMMY Sam Snead, a.k.a. the West Virginia Hillbilly, is one of golf's immortals. His alliterative nickname sprang from the verve of his personality and his style of play on the golf course. An easygoing, likable man, Snead claimed he kept all his prize money in tin cans that he buried near his West Virginia home.

SLIDING BILLY He played from 1888 to 1901, and in that time stole 912 bases. A 5'6", 165-pounder, William Robert ("Billy") Hamilton three years in a row stole over a hundred bases. His steals and his slides earned him his nickname. His reputation coupled with a .344 lifetime batting average was good enough to get him admitted to baseball's Hall of Fame in 1961.

SLINGIN' SAMMY BAUGH He came out of Texas Christian University, after having tossed a record 599 passes in three seasons, to join the Washington Redskins in 1937. Six times he led the NFL in passing; six times he was chosen All-Pro. Baugh's nickname derived from his highly accurate, rubber-armed passing over a 16-year pro career.

CONN SMYTHE TROPHY The National Hockey League's playoff Most Valuable Player award, first presented in 1964, this trophy is named after the former Toronto coach-manager-owner.

SOCCER Through the centuries some type of football has been played. The first visitors to the Polynesian Islands found the natives kicking a ball made from bamboo fibers. Early callers on the Eskimos witnessed them kicking around a leather ball that was filled with moss. The Chinese, circa 400 B.C., played *Tsu Chu,* a game in which players had to kick a ball through a hole in a silk net. "Ye Olde Football" in traced by some accounts to the Roman occupation of Britain and the British copying the Roman game of Haspastan. As the English football game evolved, and then competed with rugby football, a need to codify and clarify it was evident.

On October 26, 1863, an historic meeting took place at Freeman's Tavern in London. That conference today is viewed as the birth date of modern football, or soccer. The Football Association (F.A.) was formed. Its object was to confine itself exclusively to a kicking game, as distinct from rugby. The Football Association became and still is the ruling body of the game in England—and the only national association in the world that omits the name of its country in its official title.

Association Football became known as "association." Then it was abridged to "assoc." Ultimately the word was garbled into its present form, "soccer." To make things a bit more complex and confusing, the word *football* today is used in virtually every nation of the world to describe the sport that those in the United States refer to as "soccer."

SOFTBALL The sport was originally called kittenball

when it was played indoors with an oversized baseball in 1895. Lewis Robert, a Minneapolis firefighter, is credited with making the first softball—a softer and larger version of the ball used in baseball. It is alleged that firehouse spare-time inspired Lewis to innovate what was at first an indoor game that was played on a field with a diamond about two-thirds the size of the normal baseball diamond. By the turn of the century, the sport had moved outdoors and had a distinctive rule requiring that pitchers throw underhand. In 1933 the sport was given a new name, "softball," and was a featured part of the Century of Progress World's Fair in Chicago. Its new name came from the softness of the ball and indeed, there are today those who refer to baseball as "hardball," to distinguish the two sports.

"SOONER WITH SPOONER" In 1954 Karl Benjamin Spooner, left-handed pitcher, joined the Brooklyn Dodgers. He pitched two complete games, yielding no runs and a total of only seven hits, and amazingly, he struck out a grand total of 27 batters. The Brooklyn fans switched from their traditional slogan of "Wait 'til next year" to one that had more immediate promise, "Sooner with Spooner." Sadly, as has occurred with so many baseball phenoms, Spooner soon faded. In 1955 he won eight games and lost six, and by 1956 he was through as a major leaguer.

SOUTHEASTERN CONFERENCE This term designates the collegiate athletic conference consisting of Alabama, Auburn, Florida, Georgia, Kentucky, Louisiana State, Mississippi, Mississippi State, Tennessee, and Vanderbilt.

"SPAHN AND SAIN AND PRAY FOR RAIN" The Boston
Braves of the late 1940's were a pretty successful
baseball team. A large part of their success resulted
from the efforts of pitchers Warren Spahn and Johnny
Sain. In 1947 the dynamic duo accounted for 42 wins
between them. The following year they won a total of
39 games and powered the Braves to the National
League pennant. "There was more than Spahn and
Sain," remembers former Braves traveling secretary
Don Davidson. "There were a couple of guys named
Bobby Hogue and Nelson Potter, but hardly anybody
remembers them." The "Spahn and Sain" slogan was
actually a throwback to "Tyler, James, and Rudolph"—a slogan of the 1914 "Miracle Braves."
George Tyler, Bill James, and Dick Rudolph were the
winning pitchers in 69 of the club's 94 victories. Day
after day for 60 straight games, the trio alternated as
pitchers for that 1914 Boston Braves team (see
MIRACLE BRAVES).

SPALDEEN The name of the bouncing rubber ball that is
part of the memory of most Americans is a shortened
or "sweetened" form of Alfred Goodwill Spalding's
name (see SPALDING).

SPALDING Alfred Goodwill Spalding (1850–1915) is a
member of baseball's Hall of Fame. In 1871 he won 21
games. Then he went on to post records of 36–8,
41–15, 52–18, and 56–5. At the age of 26, in 1876,
Spalding managed the Chicago White Stockings to the
pennant and helped his own cause by winning 46
games. In 1880 he packed it in as an active major
leaguer and founded a sporting goods firm that made a

fortune—and made his name part of the language. His rigid specifications for the manufacture of baseballs gave stability and uniformity to the balls used in the sport up to that time. His name became a synonym for a baseball (see SPALDEEN).

SPLENDID SPLINTER He was also nicknamed the Thumper, because of the power with which he hit the ball, and the Kid, because of his tempestuous attitude—but his main nickname was perhaps the most appropriate. Ted Williams was one of the most splendid players who ever lived, and he could really "splinter" the ball. The handsome slugger compiled a lifetime batting average of .344 and a slugging percentage of .634. Williams blasted 521 career home runs, scored nearly 1,800 runs, and drove in over 1,800 runs. So keen was his batting eye that he walked over 2,000 times while striking out only 709 times. In 1941 he batted .406—the last time any player hit .400 or better. One of the most celebrated moments in the career of the Boston Red Sox slugger took place in the 1946 All-Star Game. Williams came to bat against Rip Sewell and his celebrated "eephus" (blooper) pitch. Williams had already walked in the game and hit a home run. Sewell's pitch came to the plate in a high arc, and Williams actually trotted out to the pitch, bashing it into the right-field bullpen for a home run. "That was the first homer ever hit off the pitch," Sewell said later.

"The ball came to the plate in a twenty-foot arc," recalled Williams. "I didn't know whether I'd be able to get enough power into that kind of a pitch for a home run." There was no kind of pitch Williams couldn't hit for a home run (see EEPHUS PITCH).

STADIUM The first Olympic footrace was run over a distance of 606 feet and nine inches. This was a Greek unit of measurement called a *stadion,* and the race was named for the unit of measurement. The stands and the viewing area together with the site where the race was staged all eventually were referred to by the word *stadion.* And the site of the first Olympics, the *stadion* at Olympia, was the forerunner of all the world's stadiums.

STANLEY CUP Frederick Arthur, Lord Stanley of Preston, Canada's governor-general in 1893, offered a trophy in his name to be awarded to the amateur hockey champs of Canada. The cost of that original trophy was $48.67. (He never saw a Stanley Cup game, for he returned to his native England before the first one was played, on March 22, 1894.) The successor of that cup is now awarded to the National Hockey League champion, and "Stanley Cup" describes the league's playoff series. Lord Stanley, incidentally, was the son of the Earl of Derby, who lent part of his name to the English Derby and the Kentucky Derby. The Stanley Cup is the oldest of all the North American competitive professional trophies (see DERBY and KENTUCKY DERBY).

STEADY EDDIE New York Yankee broadcaster Mel Allen invented this rhyming name for pitcher Eddie Lopat. A hard-working, consistent performer, Lopat led the Yankee pitching staff five years in a row in earned-run average (see JUNK MAN).

STILT, THE Wilt Chamberlain, great National Basketball Association All-Star, was one man who could make heads turn upward. Over seven feet tall, he seemed to most of the opposition and the fans to be playing on stilts, and that's where his nickname came from. Chamberlain had a 30.1 lifetime scoring average and once scored 100 points in a single game. He was also known as The Dipper, for many of his shots were simply "dipped" or dropped into the basket from above the rim. The greatest offensive player in the history of the game, Chamberlain's career began in the 1959–60 season, at a time when there were not so many dominant big men playing. Thus, his "Stilt" nickname underscored his size.

STRATFORD STREAK National Hockey League Hall of Famer Howie Morenz of the Montreal Canadiens was the sport's dominant figure during the Roaring Twenties. A speedy center with a devastating shot, Morenz scored 270 goals in his career. He had a whole collection of nicknames, as fans and the media strained to characterize him. The "Stratford Streak" title was coined for his speed and for what some thought was his birthplace, Stratford, Ontario. Actually Morenz was born in Mitchell, Ontario. Thus he got a new nickname, The Mitchell Meteor. He was also called the Marvel of Hockey and the Canadian Catapault—both referring to his skills on the ice. Quebec's French-speaking fans dubbed him *L'homme-éclair* or the Top Man. The prime of his career included 11 exciting years with Montreal. He was then traded to Chicago, and later to the New York Americans. The Canadiens got him back in 1936. On the comeback trail with Montreal, he suffered broken bones in his leg and ankle, was hospitalized, and tragically, after five weeks in the hospital, slipped and fell and died of a heart seizure. He was only 34 years old. Funeral services were held at center ice in the Montreal Forum, and thousands cried for the man they also called *Le Grande Morenz*.

SUDDEN DEATH MEL HILL He would have gone through his National Hockey League career as a relative unknown. For Mel Hill, who played in the years 1937–47 for Boston and Toronto, was a journeyman forward. But he was touched with greatness in the Stanley Cup play-offs as a member of the 1939 Boston Bruins team. In the opening game of the final series, Boston was tied, 1–1, with the New York Rangers with only 35 seconds left in a third overtime (sudden death) period. Speeding down the right side, Hill snared a pass from teammate Bill Cowley and shot the puck into the Ranger goal. Hill scored another sudden-death goal in the second game. The score was tied in the ninth minute of the first overtime when Hill got off a 30-foot shot that evaded Ranger goalie Bert Gardiner. The series moved to a seventh and decisive game. The two teams battled through regulation time, through the first overtime, the second overtime. At approximately one o'clock in the morning, eight minutes into the third sudden-death period, Hill struck again. Positioned ten feet in front of the Ranger goal, he smashed the puck in for Boston's winning score. Thus Hill scored goals in three different overtime (sudden death) games, including the seventh game's third overtime period.

SUGAR BOWL After World War II the state of Louisiana led the United States in the production of cane sugar and earned the nickname the Sugar State. The state's massive sports stadium, the Sugar Bowl, located in New Orleans, and the collegiate invitational bowl game that usually includes one team from the Southeastern Conference, derive their common name from the state's nickname.

SULLIVAN AWARD The Amateur Athletic Union award for the "amateur athlete, who, by performance, example and good influence did the most to advance the cause of good sportsmanship during the year" originated in 1930. The award is named for James E. Sullivan, AAU president for three consecutive terms and a figure largely responsible for the organization's growth and progress. Golfer Bobby Jones was the winner of the first Sullivan Award, in 1930. Other winners have included Don Budge (1937), Doc Blanchard (1945), Wilma Rudolph (1961), Mark Spitz (1971), Bill Walton (1973), and Bruce Jenner (1976).

SULTAN OF SWAT One of the nicknames given to Babe Ruth—Swat was once a principality but today is part of Pakistan (see BABE).

SUPER BOWL The merger of the American Football League and the National Football League led to the need for a championship game. The first contest was played on January 15, 1967, and although officially it was known as the National Football League championship game, its unofficial name, the Super Bowl, was used in the media, by the fans, and by the players—and the name has stuck.

One theory for how the high-sounding name came

about is that at an owner's meeting centering on a discussion of what to call the game, one of the moguls had in his pocket a super ball that he had taken away from his youngster earlier that day. The owner was not too taken with the long and ordinary-sounding suggestion for what would become pro football's ultimate game. Squeezing the ball, he suggested the name Super Bowl, but the name was not received with much enthusiasm. Nevertheless, he mentioned the name to a reporter and as they say in sporting circles, "The rest is history."

The first Super Bowl saw the first dual-network color-coverage simulcast of a sports event in history, and attracted the largest viewership ever to witness a sporting event up to that time. The Nielsen rating indicated that 73 million fans watched all or part of that game on one of the two networks, CBS or NBC. In actuality, the game was a contest between the two leagues and the two networks, for the CBS allegiance was to the NFL, and the NBC allegiance was to the American Football League, which it had virtually created with its network dollars.

The Super Bowl from the start has been designated with a Roman numeral rather than by year—a move on the part of NFL Commissioner Pete Rozelle to give the contest a sense of class, and at the same time, of continuity.

SUPERCHIEF Most major league baseball players of Indian descent somehow have been tagged with the nickname Chief. Allie Reynolds, whose glory years were 1947–54 with the New York Yankees, was no ordinary pitcher, but he was of Indian descent. Thus the man born in Bethany, Oklahoma, was nicknamed Superchief.

SUPERJEW Born April 4, 1943, in the Bronx, New York, Mike Epstein played for five different teams in an eight-year major league baseball career. His religion and his size (6′4″, 230 pounds) were the roots for his nickname.

T

TALL TACTICIAN, THE Cornelius Alexander McGilli-
cuddy, also and better known as Connie Mack, was a
major league baseball manager for 53 years. He ranks
first in games managed, games won, and games lost. A
lean, six-foot-plus individual, his size and the millions
of managing decisions he made between 1894 and
1950 earned this Hall of Famer his alliterative nickname.

TENNIS Various theories exist concerning how the game
of tennis got its name. One theory states that the
French word *tenez* is the root for the word *tennis*.
Tenez, originally spelled *tenetz,* meant "to take heed"
and in a broader sense, "to play." Other theorists
claim that the word derives from the ancient Egyptian
city of Tanis in the Nile River delta. The Arabic word

for the city was *Tinnis*. The city of Tinnis was a booming locale for the making of fine linens, and the early
tennis balls were created from light fabrics. Thus, once
upon a time there might have been *tinnis* balls.

TENNIS SCORING The unusual scoring of a game in
tennis—15 (one point), 30 (two points), 40 (three
points)—originated with the recording of the progres-
sion of the rallies, or "rests," in real tennis. These
were noted on a simple clock face positioned near the
court. A player that won a rally would have his pointer
moved through one quarter—the 15th minute. After
the next rally, the pointer would be moved to 30, or to
the next quarter on the clock. The next movement was
to the three-quarter mark, or 45. Ultimately 45 was
abbreviated to 40. When the pointer went around full-
circle, it was an indication that the conclusion of the
game had been reached.

TERRIBLE TED "I stopped counting the scars when they
reached 400," Ted Lindsay once said. He was called
Terrible and Scarface by the opposition, but there was
always a grudging respect for the 5'8", 160-pound Detroit Red Wing Hall of Famer. A vicious bodychecker,
handy with his stick or his fists if the occasion demanded it, Lindsay was a slashing, driving, frenetic
performer who made it "terribly" tough for the opposition.

**"THE BIGGER THEY ARE, THE HARDER THEY
FALL"** Bob Fitzsimmons was one of the most unusual physical specimens ever to perform in a boxing
ring. He had a heavyweight's torso, a lightweight's
head, and a middleweight's legs. During his career he

was at different times middleweight champion of the world, light-heavyweight champion of the world, and heavyweight champion of the world. The size or shape or reputation of an opponent did not faze him—he fought all comers all over the world. John L. Sullivan called him "a fighting machine on stilts" and marveled at his ability to knock out men many pounds heavier than him.

Fitzsimmons defeated Gentleman Jim Corbett for the heavyweight championship and chose Jim Jeffries as the first man to fight in defense of the crown. When critics wondered about the choice—Jeffries would outweigh Fitzsimmons by about 50 pounds, and was 13 years younger—Fitz responded, "The bigger they are, the harder they fall." Those words had worked for the English-born boxer all his life, but this fight would be different. They fought on June 9, 1899, at the Seaside Sporting Club in Coney Island. Jeffries stayed in his famous crouch. Fitzsimmons kept boring in but was unable to land any telling blows. The fifth round was the actual climax of the fight. Fitzsimmons unloaded his famous solar-plexus punch—the punch that had destroyed Corbett. Although the blow was delivered with great force right to the pit of the challenger's stomach, although Fitzsimmons moved back to give Jeffries room to topple—nothing happened. Jeffries blinked and kept on fighting. In the 11th round a new champion was crowned, as the utterly fatigued champ went down and out. Age, not size, had caught up with Bob Fitzsimmons, who fought his first bout when Jeffries was five years old.

"THE FUTURE IS NOW" When George Allen took over as head coach of the Washington Redskins of the NFL in 1971, he immediately traded for veteran players. Many of his trades involved giving up future draft choices to other teams for the immediate value of football players able to perform for Washington. Some criticized Allen, claiming he was mortgaging the future for the present. His response was that "the future is now" (see OVER-THE-HILL GANG).

"THEY NEVER COME BACK" Just who uttered what is now a phrase associated with the heavyweight division of boxing, is unknown. Its rationale is clear, though. For throughout history there have been examples of boxers—dethroned, damaged, defeated, retired—who attempted to make a comeback. Rusty, aged, out of condition, after their time, lacking motivation, these fighters, goaded by the desire for one more big pay check, one more fling in the spotlight, disappointed themselves and their fans. Thus the expression—almost a cliché—is well rooted in boxing. Such figures as Muhammad Ali have weakened the generalization. Ali came back not once but twice to claim the heavyweight championship of the world.

JIM THORPE TROPHY The annual award to the most valuable player in the National Football League is named in honor of the great Indian athlete who starred in baseball, in track, and in the Olympics. Thorpe gained national prominence in 1912 for his Olympic decathlon triumphs. In 1915 he was signed by the Canton Bulldogs of the NFL for the then-lavish fee of $250 a game. A 6'1", 190-pound power runner, it was said of

him, "When old Jim hits them, they rattle." Thorpe's
value to football transcended what he did on the field.
He was a gate attraction who enabled the sport to grow
and prosper.

THREE FINGER BROWN Hall of Famer Mordecai Peter
Centennial Brown had a mangled right hand as a result
of a childhood accident—and that was the reason for
his nickname. It was also, according to Brown, the
reason for his success as a pitcher for the Chicago Cubs
and others. "It gave me a bigger dip for my pitches,"
he said. Brown's dip helped him record 58 lifetime
shutouts and average over 24 wins a year in the 1906–
11 period, while allowing barely a run a game in the
1906 and 1909 seasons. Admitted to the Hall of Fame
in 1949, Brown's lifetime earned-run average was an
astonishing 2.06, the third lowest in baseball history.
Incidentally, his penultimate name, Centennial,
reflected the fact that he was born in the centennial
year of the United States, which was also first year of
the National League.

TINKER TO EVERS TO CHANCE A synonym for making the double play in baseball is the expression "Tinker to Evers to Chance." Yet the Chicago Cub trio,
during the peak years of their careers (1906 to 1909),
averaged less than 14 double plays a year. What they
did on the field was romanticized in the famous poem
written by Franklin P. Adams:

These are the saddest of possible words—
    "Tinker to Evers to Chance."
Trio of bear cubs, and fleeter than birds—
    "Tinker to Evers to Chance."
Ruthlessly pricking our gonfalon bubble—

Making a Giant hit into a double—
Words that are weighty with nothing but trouble:
"Tinker to Evers to Chance."

TOE, THE Lou Groza's kicking foot produced 1,343
points, on 234 field goals and 641 extra points, during
his National Football League career. His coach, Paul
Brown, said: "Lou Groza shortened the field from 100
yards to 60 yards." Perhaps the greatest place-kicker
of all time, the 6′3″, 250-pound Groza was the hub of
the Cleveland Browns during most of the 1960's. His
kicking foot was the hub of his performance skills and
it earned him an apt nickname.

**"TO PLAY THIS GAME YOU'VE GOT TO HAVE A LOT
OF LITTLE BOY IN YOU"** Hall of Famer Roy Campanella, for a decade a fixture with the Brooklyn
Dodgers, was the originator of what is now a cliché
about baseball. Campy had a lot of little boy in him,
and a great deal of major league talent. He was a
powerfully built catcher, a marvelous handler of pitch
ers, a clutch-hitting slugger, but an automobile accident curtailed his playing career and tragically reduced
him to remaining in a wheelchair for the rest of his
days. His love of baseball is reflected in his insightful
comment about the game.

TRAMPOLINE American George Nissen formally named
this gymnastic apparatus in 1926, but its name
stretches back to the circuses of the Middle Ages, in
which similar devices were used. The word *trampoline*
is derived from the Italian word for "stilt"—and stilts
were what acrobats used back then on makeshift tram-
polines.

TRICKY DICK One of the all-time greats in National Basketball Association history, Dick McGuire was one of the smoothest and most skilled of ballhandlers. His behind-the-back passes, his ability to find the open man, his feinting virtuosity, and his excellent dribbling provided the reason for his nickname.

TRIPLE CROWN (BASEBALL) A symbolic—and financially very rewarding—accomplishment achieved by a baseball player who leads his league in home runs, runs batted in, and batting average, all in the same season.

TRIPLE CROWN (ENGLISH HORSE RACING) A feat accomplished by a thoroughbred who wins the Derby, the Two Thousand Guineas, and the St. Leger in the same year.

TRIPLE CROWN (HARNESS RACING) A trotter who wins the Hambletonian, the Kentucky Futurity, and the Yonkers Trot in the same season gains harness-racing's Triple Crown.

TRIPLE CROWN (HORSE RACING) A feat achieved by a three-year-old thoroughbred who wins the Kentucky Derby, the Preakness, and the Belmont Stakes in the same year. The winning of the Acorn, the Mother Goose Stakes, and the Coaching Club of America Stakes in the same season is regarded as the Triple Crown for fillies, since generally they do not compete against colts.

TRIPLE CROWN (PACING) This accomplishment involves a pacer winning the Little Brown Jug, the Cane Pace, and the Messenger Stakes in the same season.

TUG Frank Edwin McGraw, Jr., left-handed relief pitcher, coauthor of a comic strip called *Scroogie,* possessor of a wicked screwball, and in his own words, "a little bit of a screwball myself," is a baseball original. McGraw was a member of the New York Mets from 1967 to 1974. In back-to-back years, 1971 and 1972, his earned-run average was a glittering 1.70. He starred for the Mets in two World Series and coined the slogan of the team back then, "Ya Gotta Believe." His parents named him Tug because he tugged at so many things when he was a baby (see "YA GOTTA BELIEVE").

U-V

VARDON GRIP Named for golfing great Harry Vardon, and also known as the overlapping grip, this is the grip employed by most top golfers. Vardon's actual description of what he did is as follows: "The right hand is brought up so high that the palm of it covers over the left thumb, leaving very little of the latter to be seen. The first and second fingers of the right hand just reach round to the thumb of the left and the third finger completes the overlapping process, so that the club is held in the grip as if it were in a vice. The little finger of the right hand rides on the first finger of the left" (see VARDON TROPHY).

VARDON TROPHY Golf's award for the performer with the lowest average each year on the pro tour is named for Harry Vardon, six-time British Open winner and

one-time United States Open champ. The first Vardon
Trophy winner was Sam Snead in 1950 with a 69.23
average, which to date has not been topped (see
VARDON GRIP).

VEZINA TROPHY The National Hockey League's award
for the leading goalkeeper was first presented in
1926–27 by the owners of the Montreal franchise, in
honor of their former star goalkeeper, Georges Vezina
(see CHICOUTIMI CUCUMBER).

VOLLEYBALL William G. Morgan, director of the
Y.M.C.A. of Holyoke, Massachusetts, and a
Springfield College student, is credited with inventing
the sport of volleyball and giving it its name. He actually originated a game that he called Mintonette. In
1895 he began to experiment with variations of this
game. Experiments with a net and a ball encouraged
his students to volley the ball over the net, which led to
their volleying the ball and resulting in Morgan's
changing the name of the sport from Mintonette to
volleyball.

W

"WAIT 'TIL NEXT YEAR" A plantive refrain echoed annually by the fans of the old Brooklyn Dodgers, this
phrase was an expression of eternal optimism and faith
in the ability of their beloved bums to make up for all
the failures and inadequacies of years gone by. It especially applied to the World Series. In 1941, for example, the Dodgers won the pennant but lost the World
Series in five games to the New York Yankees. In
1947 the Dodgers won the pennant and lost again in the
World Series, this time in seven games, to the New
York Yankees. They lost in the 1949 World Series to
the Yankees; they bowed in the 1952 World Series to
the Yankees; they were defeated in the 1953 World
Series by the Yankees—but 1955 was "next year."
The series went seven games, and the Dodgers de-

feated the New York Yankees and became World Champions at long last.

WALKER CUP George A. Walker, former president of the United States Golf Association, donated a trophy for an international annual golf competition. The newspapers called the trophy the Walker Cup. Walker's plan evolved into a British-American golfing competition that after being held annually in 1922, 1923, and 1924, became a biennial event. Today the competition involves four 18-hole matched foursomes and eight 18-hole singles matches.

WALKING MAN, THE Eddie Yost played nearly two decades in the major leagues. His lifetime batting average was only .254, but that didn't keep him off the bases. Yost coaxed pitchers into yielding 1,614 walks to him—almost a walk a game through his long career—which places him fifth on the all-time bases-on-balls list.

WEE WILLIE He was born March 3, 1872, in Brooklyn, New York. He died on January 1, 1923, in Brooklyn, New York. His name was William Henry Keeler. A lefty all the way, he weighed only 140 pounds and was a shade over 5'4". His tiny physical stature earned him his nickname, but pound for pound he was one of the greatest hitters baseball ever produced. Keeler played for 19 years and recorded a lifetime batting average of .345, fifth on the all-time list. He collected 2,962 hits in 2,124 games, spraying the ball to all fields. Wee Willie's greatest year was 1897, a season in which he batted .432, recorded 243 hits and 64 stolen bases, and scored 145 runs. He swung a bat that weighed only 30 ounces, but as he said, he "hit 'em where they ain't" —and that was more than good enough to gain Keeler entry into baseball's Hall of Fame in 1939 (see "HIT 'EM WHERE THEY AIN'T").

WELTERWEIGHT BOXING DIVISION The word *welter* was originally used to describe a weight class in English horse racing. About 1792, English boxers who weighed around 145 pounds referred to themselves as "welters." Paddington Tom Jones was the first "welterweight" champion; from 1792 to 1795, Jones triumphed in matches against all challengers.

WHIP, THE A 6'6" right-hander, Ewell Blackwell had a sidearm motion and a crackling fastball that terrorized National League batters in the 1940's and 1950's. The former Cincinnati star's right arm seemed to "whip" the ball in at the batter, and that's how his nickname came to be. Winner of sixteen straight games in 1947, he struck out almost a batter an inning during his ten-year career.

WHIZ KIDS There is no clear explanation as to how the 1950 Philadelphia Phillies baseball team earned its nickname. Some ascribe the name's derivation to the club's youth and newness: only one regular on that team that won the National League pennant was over 30 years of age. Some claim the nickname was a spin-off from the phrase "gee whiz," since the Phillies of that year seemingly came from nowhere to challenge and defeat the great Brooklyn Dodgers for the pennant. It was a team that because of its youth, its underdog role, and its past history of failure, attracted national attention and fused its personality to its nickname.

WIGHTMAN CUP Mrs. George Wightman, the former Helen Hotchkiss, was the American national singles tennis champion from 1909 to 1911. The cup named for her was donated by Mrs. Wightman in 1923 for competition between teams of women players from the United States and England. The first contest was held at Forest Hills, New York.

WILD BULL OF THE PAMPAS, THE Luis Angel Firpo was a 6'3", 220-pound boxer from Argentina. His wild hair, his bobbing head as he sprung from his corner to start a round, and his Argentinian ancestry prompted the nickname given to him by writer Damon Runyon. Firpo and his nickname are both especially remembered as a result of his September 14, 1923, Polo Grounds battle with Jack Dempsey. The epic slugfest lasted only to the 57th second of the second round. Up to that point, Dempsey had been downed twice by Firpo, while the Manassa Mauler had pounded Firpo to the mat six times. Firpo fought in a fury, like a wild bull, like a wild and maimed bull. The fight ended in the 57th second of that second round, when Dempsey put him down for the seventh and final time.

WILD HORSE OF THE OSAGE, THE Johnny Leonard Roosevelt Martin, better known as Pepper Martin, starred for 13 seasons with the National League's St. Louis Cardinals. He could hit, he could run, he could field, he could throw, he could win—and he did all of these things with wild abandon, with an elan and a verve that earned him his nickname. If he couldn't stop a hard smash down to his third-base position with his glove, he would stop the ball with his chest. If he could

not get into a base feet-first, he would leap into the air
and belly-flop his way there. Martin took the extra
base, risked the daring chance, played with fire and
fury. Three times in the mid-1930's he led the league
in stolen bases, and throughout that decade he
functioned as the horse that led the Cardinal "Gashouse Gang" (see GASHOUSE GANG).

WIMBLEDON One day in 1877, three British sportsmen
were taking a leisurely walk past the All-England
Croquet Club. Julian Marshall, Henry Jones, and
C. G. Heathcote allegedly marveled at the fine grass
and decided that the locale was a perfect spot for a
lawn tennis competition. They enlisted the aid of J. H.
Walsh, influential editor of the *Field Magazine* to get
the All-England Croquet Club to change its name to
the All-England Croquet and Lawn Tennis Club and to
introduce tennis into the program. The birth of the
British National Tennis Tournament took place in a
notice that was posted on June 9, 1877: "The All-
England Croquet and Lawn Tennis Club, Wimbledon,
propose to hold a lawn tennis meeting open to all
amateurs on Monday July 9 and following days. En-
trance fee, one shilling. Two prizes will be given—one
gold champion prize to the winner, one silver to the
second player." The rules that governed that tournament specified a rectangular court 26 yards long and
nine yards wide and a net that extended from poles
three feet outside the court. One service fault without
penalty was permitted: scoring was done by "15s," as
opposed to the 1-2-3-4 formula for racquets. These
rules formed the foundation for tennis for nearly 100

years. Until 1968, the tournament was open only to amateurs, but that year it became the first major tournament to switch to open competition. The name Wimbledon comes from the site, Wimbledon Park, a suburb outside of London.

"WINNING ISN'T EVERYTHING—IT'S THE ONLY THING" In 1959 Vince Lombardi took over as head coach of the Green Bay Packers. The year before, the Pack had lost ten games, tied one, and won one. Lombardi announced, "I'm in command here." He moved Green Bay in his first season as coach to a record of seven wins and five losses. By 1960 Lombardi, pushing, driving, scheming, inspiring, steered the Green Bay team to the Western Division National Football League title. In 1961 the Packers recorded their first World Championship in 17 years. There was another championship in 1962, another in 1965, and another in 1966. The first Super Bowl ever played was a personal victory for Lombardi, as his Green Bay team demolished Kansas City, 35–10, on January 15, 1967. The following year, in Super Bowl II, Green Bay triumphed over Oakland, 33–14, in Lombardi's final game as Packer coach. Lombardi transformed the Packers from chronic losers into perennial winners during his nine glorious seasons as their coach, and he made his slogan into a way of life for the players and the fans of Green Bay (see "GETTING A TIE IS LIKE KISSING YOUR SISTER").

"WIN ONE FOR THE GIPPER" Storied Notre Dame Football player George Gipp died at the age of 23, at the height of his powers. Famed Notre Dame coach

Knute Rockne related how Gipp in his deathbed speech said, "Sometime, Rock, when the team's up against it, when things are wrong and the breaks are beating the boys, tell them to go in there with all they've got and win just one for the Gipper. . . . " Rockne used that story to psyche up his Notre Dame players again and again. The phrase has become part of the language of inspirational sports expressions.

WORLD CUP Perhaps the ultimate in sports competition, soccer's World Championship eclipses baseball's World Series, football's Super Bowl, hockey's Stanley Cup, and horse racing's Triple Crown. It is held at a different site every four years midway between Olympic years. More than 100 nations today compete for up to two years to qualify for the finals, which are staged over a two- to three-week period in the summer. The host nation and the reigning World Cup champion automatically qualify. The 14 survivors of the competition join with these two to complete the field of 16. Amateurs, professionals, and naturalized citizens of a country are eligible to participate. The concept of the World Cup was inspired by the dissatisfaction of some European nations, who claimed the Olympic Games placed them at a disadvantage in vying for a world soccer title. These nations reasoned that the Olympics were restricted to amateurs and their best players were professionals. Jules Rimet, a leading figure in French soccer and the president of Fédération International de Football (FIFA), the ruling body of the sport, together with Henri Delauney, another leading French soccer personality, conceived the basic outline and structure of the World Cup. Uruguay won the first World Cup, which was held in 1930.

WORLD SERIES In 1903 the Pittsburgh Pirates of the National League won their third consecutive pennant. Owner Barney Dreyfuss was instrumental in arranging for a set of postseason games with the American League champion Boston Somersets (later Red Sox). The teams played a nine-game series, with Boston winning five of the games (one of their pitchers was Cy Young) and the World Championship. There was a one-year interruption in the competition, because the 1904 National League pennant-winner was the New York Giants, whose owner, John T. Bush, refused to allow his team to oppose an American League entry. Part of the reason behind Bush's refusal was the existence of a rival American League team in New York City. By 1905 Bush had changed his mind and even helped shape the new format for the World Series—a best-of-seven competition—and behind Christy Mathewson, who pitched three shutouts, the Giants defeated the Philadelphia Athletics in five games. Dubbed the Fall Classic, the World Series year in and year out has become an integral, appealing part of the American sports scene.

WRIGLEY FIELD In 1916 William Wrigley, Jr., joined with a group of wealthy Chicagoans to purchase the Chicago Cubs. The National League team was thus wrested from the absentee ownership of the Taft family of Cincinnati. In 1921 Wrigley took over the major ownership of the team. By 1926 the old Federal ball park that the Cubs played in was given a new name in honor of its owner—Wrigley Field. The park was double-decked, freshly painted, and renovated. And through the years, the ball park and the Cubs have been synonymous with the Wrigley family. The past is as real as the present at Wrigley Field, on the North Side of Chicago. All the games are played in daylight on grass that is real and green. Ivy vines cover the red-brick outfield walls. Tall buildings crowd close to the little ball park, serving as penthouse seats for the Cub rooters. There is no electric scoreboard, no advertising. The oldest stadium in the National League, the field and its mood have the stamp of the Wrigleys, as well as the name.

WRONG WAY RIEGELS An astonished crowd at the 1929 Rose Bowl watched Roy Riegels, University of California, run 70 yards to his own end zone before he was finally brought down by a teammate. Riegels, who forever will be known as Wrong Way Reigels for his odd run, maintained, "At least I was trying."

X-Y-Z

YACHTING The roots of this sport can be traced back to the Dutch word *jaght,* which means to "put on speed." *Jaghtschips* were speedy cargo boats that made their way over the Dutch canals and sometimes engaged in sporting races. In 1660 King Charles II left to take over the British throne and was given a yacht as a gift by the Dutch government. A couple of years later, King Charles II raced his yacht against one owned by the Duke of York. The king won the race, and the sport was on its way to winning the hearts of the seafaring English.

"YA GOTTA BELIEVE" In 1973 the New York Mets bolted from last place on August 30 to win the National League Eastern Division title on the final day of the season. Pitcher Tug McGraw had coined a slogan, "Ya gotta believe," which acted as the team's battle cry and motivation. Lacking a .300 hitter, a 20-game winner, a 100-RBI man, the "believing" Mets swept by Cincinnati in the play-offs and battled Oakland to the seventh game of the World Series before finally losing (see AMAZIN' METS).

YANKEE CLIPPER In 16 seasons for the New York Yankees, Joe DiMaggio compiled a .325 batting average and a .579 slugging precentage. Like the famed Yankee clipper ships that sailed the oceans riding the winds and the tides, DiMaggio moved across the reaches of the center-field pastureland of Yankee Stadium flawlessly playing his kind of game—steady, stoical, dependable. His nickname accentuated his role and style. DiMaggio was also known as Jolting Joe because of his power, and Joe Di, an affectionate abbreviation of his name.

YEAR OF THE RUNNER During the 1972 National Football League season, for the first time in history ten runners rushed for 1,000 yards or more. That year in pro football was named for them and later rules changes stemmed from their domination of the sport that year.

"YOU COULD LOOK IT UP" Casey Stengel began his major league playing career in 1912, his managing career in 1934. He played for 14 years, managed for 25 years. His baseball career ended in 1965 after stints with the Brooklyn Dodgers, Boston Braves, Pittsburgh Pirates, Philadelphia Phillies, New York Giants, New York Yankees, New York Mets. Casey could talk for hours about baseball and life. And sometimes in the midst of animated conversation about a utility outfielder on the old Boston Braves, or a balk by a forgotten pitcher on the Pittsburgh Pirates—to emphasize that he was not relating fiction he would exclaim: "You could look it up!"

CY YOUNG AWARD Baseball's award to the top pitcher in each league originated in 1956. The rationale was that pitchers were at a disadvantage in Most Valuable Player balloting. The award gets its name from the Hall of Famer who pitched for 22 years, winning more games than any other performer in baseball history (508). Young also started more games, completed more games, pitched more innings than any other pitcher in history. He is fourth on the all-time list in strikeouts and shutouts. His career accomplishments personified the value of a pitcher to a team and underlined the reason for naming the award for the top pitcher after him.

YOUTH OF AMERICA Casey Stengel's beginning years as manager of the New York Mets were a time of trial and frustration for many. Afflicted with over-the-hill players and has-beens, Casey delighted in the potential of some of the younger Mets. Although not quite ready for prime-time baseball, they had promise and Stengel's feeling for them was revealed in this phrase, which he pronounced, "The yuth of America" (see "CAN'T ANYBODY HERE PLAY THIS GAME?").

INDEX

An avid observer of the sporting scene, Harvey Frommer is a true sports generalist. He has spent the last few years getting at the root of things as a writer on sports and culture. Dr. Frommer's Ph.D. thesis explored the inter-relationship among sports, media and society. His Sports Lingo *focused on language usage in more than fifty sports. Dr. Frommer has completed a book on soccer soon to be published by Atheneum and is presently at work on a book on New York City baseball during the 1940's and 50's.*

ADDENDUM

At press time, many people suggested additional entries for *Sports Roots*. Marv Albert wondered whether YES had been included, and Red Barber fans asked about BEDFORD AVENUE BLAST and F.O.B. Someone suggested the inclusion of a survey of all the WHITEYs, the REDs, the BABEs, the BOBOs, etc. There was not enough space for these, or for the dozens of trophies, team names, expressions, competitions that exist and continue to develop in the ever-changing world of sports.

A *Sports Roots II* is being planned. I welcome suggestions and anecdotes from readers. Please send them to me % Atheneum Publishers, 122 East 42nd Street, New York, N.Y. 10017. You will be credited for everything you submit.

Thanks for your *Sportsroot*ing interest.

Harvey Frommer